Table of Contents

		Page No.
	Preface	
I.	Introductory Summary	1
	A. An Approach	3
	B. Living Costs	6
	C. Income Inequality	9
	D. Nutrition	11
	E. Poverty	12
	F. Conclusion	14
II.	Regional and Urban-Rural Variations in Living Costs	20
	A. Food Prices	23
	B. Non-Food Prices	28
	C. Overall Prices	35
III.	Spatial Inequality of Income	35
	A. Nominal Expenditures	38
	B. Real Expenditures	41
	1. Food Consumption	42
	2. Non-Food Consumption	44
	3. Total Consumption	45
IV.	Nutritional Adequacy	49
	A. Nutritional Norms	50
	B. Achievement of Norms	51
V.	Differences in Poverty Within Brazil	54
	A. Food Costs	55
	1. Type A Food Basket	56
	2. Type B Food Basket	57
	3. Type C Food Basket	58
	B. Non-Food Cost and Poverty Lines	58
	C. Income Distribution	59
	D. Poverty Measures	61
	Annex Tables	69-87
	References	88-91
	Map	

The views and interpretations in this document are those of the author and should not be attributed to the World Bank, to its affiliated organizations, or to any individual acting in their behalf.

WORLD BANK

Staff Working Paper No. 505

February 1982

DIFFERENCES IN INCOME, NUTRITION AND POVERTY WITHIN BRAZIL

Regional disparities in living standards within Brazil have received increasing attention in recent years. This paper attempts to throw light on this issue by providing a quantitative range for these differences. Drawing on the national consumption survey called ENDEF for 1974/75, estimates are set out for real income, nutritional levels and poverty for major regions, and urban and rural areas.

The results of this study indicate that, although cost of living adjustments narrow spatial differences, large regional disparities remain, particularly upon comparing the Northeast and the Southeast. The use of cost of living indices reduces urban-rural variations more than in the case of regional differences, drastically narrowing the urban-rural gap in food consumption. Poverty is, nevertheless, much more concentrated in the rural areas than in urban areas, although regional differences in the incidence of poverty are more striking than the urban-rural divergencies.

Prepared by: Vinod Thomas
              Development Economics Department
              Development Policy Staff

Copyright © 1982
The World Bank
1818 H Street, N.W.
Washington, D.C. 20433, U.S.A.

PREFACE

In recent years, increasing concern has been expressed that certain regions and areas in Brazil have been by-passed by the process of economic growth. While the visible poverty in these places lends support to this view, the need has emerged for a fuller evaluation of this issue. The results of a 1974/75 nation-wide survey called ENDEF, published from 1978 onwards, provide a basis for a comprehensive comparison of the major regions and areas.

Analysis of the ENDEF data is being carried out at other institutions as well as at FIBGE, the statistical institute in Rio de Janeiro that undertook the survey. This work was carried out at FIPE in Sao Paulo, as part of the institute's ongoing work on urban and regional poverty related studies. The research benefited from the work of several people at FIPE, in particular, Antonio Campino, Vera Fava, Roberto Macedo, Eleuterio Prado and Eduardo Solorzano. Solorzano's Master's thesis (March 1981) was in the same area of investigation, and this paper would not have been possible without the results jointly produced by him. Helpful comments were provided by Luis Ablas, Alexandre Berndt, Douglas Keare, Constantino Lluch, Paulo de Tarso Medeiros and Francisco de Assis Moura. Any errors in this paper are, of course, my responsibility.

DIFFERENCES IN INCOME, NUTRITION AND POVERTY
WITHIN BRAZIL

I. Introductory Summary

Disparity in the living standards across Brazil has been a matter of increasing concern. It is seldom disputed that the rapid economic growth during the postwar years 1/ must have brought benefits to lagging regions and areas. But it is widely held that the growth process has been very uneven. Today large spatial inequalities in well-being persist, as symbolized by the wealth evident in some areas (particularly the highly built-up urban centers of the Southeast) and the visible poverty in others.

Table I.1 compares Brazil with the rest of the world on the basis of some welfare indicators. The growth rate of the Brazilian economy surpasses the average for most of the country groups. Compared to other developing countries 2/, Brazil also performs better in terms of a number of socio-economic indicators. These indicators, doctor per population, percentage achievement of calorie requirement, etc., however, reflect welfare levels at the mean for the country as a whole. A more

---

1/ Over the past three decades, the Brazilian economy grew at an annual rate of roughly 7% in real terms. The growth rate between 1969-73 was 11%.

2/ Low income and middle income countries (to which Brazil belongs) and petroleum exporters are included in these comparisons.

disaggregated picture is presented in Tables I.2 and I.3. Although the latter tables are not fully comparable with Table I.1 owing to differences in definitions and years compared, they nevertheless suggest that indicators at the mean are quite unrepresentative for large parts of the country. Wide disparities in the availability of services and welfare levels emerge.

Thus, while Brazil as a whole has far greater numbers of doctors per population than the average for middle income countries, the situation in the Northeast (Region V - see Map 1) is not much better than in India at its <u>mean</u>. The Northeast contains 32% of the country's people (Annex Table 1). Similarly, although Brazil's mean calorie intake relative to requirements is about the same as the average middle income country, calorie deficits comparable to those in some low income countries are shown in several regions <u>1</u>/. To consider yet another indicator, while the adult literacy rate for Brazil exceeds the average for middle income countries, the estimate for the country's Northeast corresponds to the average for low income countries.

This study addresses the question of the extent of the type of disparities noted above by providing a quantitative range of the differences in well-being in Brazil. For this purpose, estimates are

---

<u>1</u>/ Deficits in Table I.2 would be larger than in Table I.1 anyway, since the former uses stricter requirements based on NRC [29] (see Section IV), while the latter (WDR estimates) are based on FAO/WHO requirements [7].

developed on income, nutrition and poverty for major regions and areas across the country. In so doing, some frequently-used approaches to measuring welfare are refined and applied.

A. An Approach

The paper draws on the results of a 1974/75 nation-wide household expenditure study (Estudo Nacional da Despesa Familiar - ENDEF). The study divides the country into seven major geographical regions on the basis of the size of their populations and their internal similarities. Most regions are further divided into one or more metropolitan areas, non-metropolitan urban areas and rural areas. Annex Tables 1 and 2 and Map 1 set out the ENDEF classification of regions and areas [1].

ENDEF surveys annual family expenditures on highly disaggregated consumption categories. The survey provides the greatest detail for food items; consumption expenditure of some 120 of these items is given separately. Intake of calories, proteins and other nutrients is also measured, which can be compared against various established nutritional norms.

Aggregates of estimated current expenditures on food and non-food items are used as measures of nominal income. Market values are imputed for non-monetary components within these measures. ENDEF reports family

---

[1] A full description of the survey method and interpretation of results can be found in [12] and [13].

expenditures, numbers of families and family sizes for nine expenditure classes. This permits us to present per capita mean expenditure values, and also approximate per capita values for people belonging to a particular percentile position in the expenditure distribution 1/. Apart from the mean, we have chosen to compare people at the 40th percentile. While representing a lower income group, this percentile also avoids problems of data inconsistency found at lower percentiles.

The data for the nine family expenditure classes are utilized to approximate continuous nominal expenditure distributions in the form of Lorenz curves. Apart from providing income concentration comparisons, these expenditure distributions enable us to measure the incidence of poverty. Against the expenditure distributions, estimated poverty lines are used to read off the number of people considered poor. Also measured is the extent to which the incomes of the poor fall short of poverty thresholds.

The poverty lines are built up from the cost of purchasing a basket of what may be considered basic need food items. As in other similar studies, nutritional requirements serve as a basis for estimating the minimum food needs, while the actual non-food/food expenditure ratio of a given low income group indicates the non-food needs.

1/ The latter is an approximation, since family sizes sometimes vary in the neighborhood of the given percentile, making a difference for expenditure classifications of the population according to whether a family or per capita measure is used.

Whether in constructing poverty lines or in comparing expenditure levels, nominal magnitudes are deflated by location-specific cost-of-living indices. Use of these price indices enables us to represent income and poverty differences more accurately than otherwise. The overall price index for any location relative to a national average is a weighted average of food and non-food price indices. The food price index is estimated directly from the ENDEF data on food expenditures and quantities consumed. A non-food price index, on the other hand, is approximated from the expenditure data, since no estimates of quantities are available. Considering the tentative nature of this index, some sensitivity tests were performed, and a lower and upper bound provided for poverty measures based on them.

The approach for estimating the non-food price index is to apply indirectly estimated income and price elasticities of demand for non-food (indirectly from the food elasticities) to separate out what must be the quantity difference in consumption while going from a hypothetical national average location to any other place. The expenditure difference remaining after separating out this quantity difference is attributed to price variation. This method tends to include, in price differences, all changes in non-food expenses, other than those occurring due to income and price changes from the national average. Thus, additional expense on a location specific need in an urban area (greater commuting, for instance) is part of the price difference. This type of accounting may, in cases, overstate price differences, and consequently help to understate the real expenditure or poverty variations between urban and rural areas. Some independent estimates of housing price differences are also provided.

Cost-of-living indices are derived at the mean and the 40th percentile alternatively using solely monetary expenditure and both monetary and non-monetary expenditures. While the indices at the mean clearly refer to qualitatively different consumption baskets across regions, the comparisons at the 40th percentile presumably reduce this problem. The inclusion of non-monetary components allows for a fuller range of the price variation. Thus, the real magnitudes at the 40th percentile based on monetary and non-monetary expenditure items are the most appropriate ones for interregional comparisons. Such comparisons as were possible in this paper represent one of the improvements in this study over a previous one for Peru [43], the overall approach of which is applied and extended for Brazil in this study.

B. Living Costs

Section II presents estimates of spatial differences in food, non-food and overall prices. In the case of food, first, a price index at the mean is first calculated for deflating the mean nominal expenditure. Second, a price index roughly at the 40th percentile [1] is presented for use in constructing poverty lines. The latter appears to be a better indicator of food price differences, since under it much of the quality differences at the mean are presumably eliminated. In each of these cases spatial differences are augmented with the inclusion of non-monetary consumption items. The rural situation is more accurately represented by the inclusion of the usually cheaper items which are not bought in the market and which are more important in the rural areas.

Significant regional price variation is brought out for a composite basket of food items consumed at the national mean. The highest prices, 11% to 21% above the national average, are observed in Regions I, II and VI, which contain the metropolitan areas of Rio, Sao Paulo and Brasilia respectively. Region VII, or the North, has comparable or higher prices, but with the exclusion of rural areas, this region is not quite comparable with the rest. Unfavorable production conditions and high transportation costs from producing areas are, nevertheless, reflected in these prices. Average or less than average prices are shown for the relatively less urbanized regions IV and V. Region III is moderately urbanized and has less than average prices, as explained by this region's importance as an agricultural producer.

---

[1] See Annex Table 3 for a description.

Food price indices rise in going from the rural to the more urbanized regions. Based on food expenditure (monetary plus non-monetary expenditure) at the 20th percentile, the state of Rio de Janeiro (Region I), the state of Sao Paulo (Region II), and Brasilia (Region VI), where the percentages of urban population are high, show price levels that are 20-40% above the national average. The Northeast (Region V) and the Centereast (Region IV), on the other hand, are less urbanized and show a moderate price level. To these and the remaining regional comparisons, the Frontier (Region VII) is not quite comparable since, as already stated, rural areas are excluded. Urban-rural differences are more clearly brought out in the comparison of the metropolitan average with the rural average for the country as a whole. About a 30% above-average price for the former contrasts with a more than 20% below-average price for the latter.

Greater urban and regional variations are found in the case of non-food than food. The non-food price indices are tentative and subject to the caveats mentioned in Section II.B. Comparisons at the 40th percentile seem reasonable, however, as some of the problems due to quality variations are presumably removed. The results for the 40th percentile are generally consistent with some independent estimates of housing prices, as well as other scattered evidence and the opinion of people familiar with the situation. Regions I, II and VI have prices well above the average; with prices in their metropolitan areas, Rio, Sao Paulo and Brasilia, are respectively 94%, 107% and 56% above average. Comparing

Region II with the more rural Region V, a 70% average price difference is noted. A full calculation of rural prices has not been possible due to data inconsistencies; but available results imply a metropolitan-rural difference of about 100% for most regions.

Based on overall prices (i.e. weighted average of food and non-food), we find higher costs of living in the apparently more affluent and urbanized locations. Metropolitan Sao Paulo's prices are estimated to be about 100% higher than the state's rural prices. Region II's prices are roughly 50% higher than Region IV's. Metropolitan prices exceed the national average by over 50%, while non-metropolitan urban prices correspond roughly to the national average.

C. Income Inequality

Locational differences in per capita nominal expenditures are very large, if cost-of-living differences are not accounted for, as reported in Section II.A. The wealthiest regions in nominal terms are Regions I, II and VI. Mean expenditures in these regions are about 50% above the national average. The metropolitan areas of Rio, Sao Paulo and Brasilia largely account for this. Regions IV and V are worst off with mean expenditures of roughly 20% and 50% below the average. The income positions of the rural areas in these regions largely account for this. In general, metropolitan areas have roughly twice the mean national average while rural areas have less than half. Non-metropolitan urban areas' expenditure roughly corresponds to the average.

The above comparisons are based on total, i.e. monetary plus non-monetary, expenditures. The use of total expenditure results in smaller divergencies than monetary expenditures alone, since non-monetary items are relatively more important in the more rural locations. Comparisons at the 40th percentile of the expenditure distribution, as opposed to the mean, also lower the spatial differences. The reason for this, according to the ENDEF, is lower concentration of income in the more rural areas 1/.

The more affluent locations spend the bulk of their additional income on non-food. Yet, in absolute terms there exist considerable differences in nominal expenses on food as well. These food expenditure differences are, however, sharply reduced (and sometimes reversed) when nominal magnitudes are deflated by price indices. In the case of non-food, on the other hand, large spatial differences remain even in real terms. Real variations for food and non-food total expenditures are discussed in Section III.B.

In real terms, regional differences in food consumption may not be very large. According to rough estimates for the 40th percentile of the expenditure distribution, some of the less urbanized areas appear to do as well or better than others. Nevertheless, consumption differences due to

---

1/ Rural landowners who live in cities form part of the city's income distribution, which may partly explain the better rural income distribution.

wide income variations across locations clearly persist. For instance, on average, the low-income Northeast achieves only 71% of the consumption in the high-income Sao Paulo state.

In the case of non-food, the more affluent and more urbanized locations fare much better in real terms, whether we compare the mean or the 40th percentile. In the latter case, the highly urbanized regions, I, II, and VI, consume 100-150% more in real terms than the Northeast. On the whole, metropolitan and urban consumption exceeds rural consumption significantly.

Summing up results on food and non-food, we obtain total consumption differences in real terms, most of which are due to differences in non-food consumption. At the mean, estimated metropolitan consumption exceeds other urban areas' consumption and rural areas' consumption systematically. Comparing the 40th percentile, these differences may be much smaller, with estimated consumption in metropolitan areas as a whole being only 2% above that in other urban areas, and 27% above that in rural areas.

D. Nutrition

In Section IV two alternative sets of nutritional norms are used to evaluate nutritional adequacy. The first set provided by ENDEF consistently states lower minimum requirements than the second derived by Campino [4] from requirements established by the National Research

Council (USA). Consequently, two quite different pictures of the overall nutritional position emerge. Based on ENDEF, the nation as a whole shows a 5% calorie surplus. Based on Campino, a 3% deficit is indicated.

Spatial differences are small according to ENDEF. Based on Campino, on the other hand, larger regional differences emerge. Calorie deficits of 8-15% are shown for Regions I, V, VI and VII in contrast with a 4-5% surplus for Regions II, III and IV. Urban-rural differences are small, on the other hand, varying from a 5% deficit in metropolitan areas, a 4% deficit in other urban areas and a 3% surplus in rural areas.

The type of urban-regional differences noted above reflect only levels of caloric intake, which are consistent with findings on real food consumption for lower income groups. The wealthier regions clearly fare better than the poorer ones in their nutritional status. The nutritional situation based on caloric adequacy is no worse in the rural areas than in the more urbanized locations.

E. Poverty

Section V brings together estimated living costs, measures of food and non-food needs and income distribution data to measure poverty. Absolute poverty thresholds are constructed that take into account: (i) nutritional needs, (ii) "minimum" non-food allowances, and (iii) their cost differences. We focus on "medium" and "low" lines, excluding those that are "high." Admittedly somewhat arbitrary, these are considered to give "medium" and "low" poverty thresholds. We have purposely adopted what may be thought of as conservative measures of poverty on grounds that they may be more useful for policy.

A first poverty measure tells us the percentage and number of people considered poor in each location. Irrespective of the poverty line chosen, the bulk of the problem is in the Northeast and the rural areas. On a "medium" poverty definition, over 29% of the nation's population is considered poor. Nearly 50% of the Northeast would be poor according to this definition. About half of the country's poor live in the Northeast. Based on the same definition, about 20% in the state of Sao Paulo are poor, constituting about 15% of the nation's poor. About 17% of the metropolitan population fall below this poverty line, in comparison with about 23% in other urban areas and about 39% in rural areas. "Low" poverty lines would remove about 10-20% of the poor from the definition.

Combining the results of the percentage of poor with estimates of the average poverty gap (i.e. income shortfall) and its distribution among the poor, an index suggested by Sen [36] is constructed to give a fuller measure of poverty. To the extent that the income distribution is worse in the poorer regions, the "Sen index" brings out larger disparities. The relative position of the rural areas is improved to the extent that the ENDEF shows a better income distribution in these areas compared to the urban ones. An alternative measure of income deficiency is given in Thomas [43] by expressing the poverty gap as a fraction of each location's income and multiplying it by the percentage of poor people. This measure indicates the percentage increase in the location's total income needed over the existing situation, with all this increase going to the poor, to eliminate poverty. Based on the "medium" definition of poverty, it is suggested that over a 5% increase in the national income is needed, with a 10% increase in the Northeast and less than 2% in the state of Sao Paulo, to remove the income deficiency of the poor.

F. Conclusion

Estimated cost of living indices vary widely within Brazil, ranging roughly from 150 or more in the cities of Sao Paulo, Rio de Janeiro and Brasilia (compared to a national average of 100) to about 100 in the majority of small towns, and less than 90 in all rural areas. These price differentials imply considerable variations in the purchasing power across the country, but even after accounting for these, large regional and urban-rural differences in the standard of living persist.

Comparing expenditure estimates, the divergencies narrow considerably with the inclusion of non-monetary expenditure items, and with comparisons at the 40th percentile of the expenditure distribution as opposed to the mean.

For a lower income group defined as belonging to the 40th percentile, expenditure in real terms in the metropolitan areas exceeds that in other urban areas by an estimated 2%, and in rural areas by 27%. Living standards of this income group in the medium-sized cities and towns (places over 50,000 people that are not considered metropolitan areas) are comparable to those in the metropolitan areas in real terms. Regional differences, on the other hand, are large. People at the 40th percentile in the state of Sao Paulo, for instance, are estimated to be twice as well off as the Northeast in real terms.

In the case of food, the application of price indices removes a large part of the urban-rural expenditure differences. In fact, the poor in many rural areas may be achieving comparable or better nutritional intake than their urban counterparts. Across regions, however, food intake does vary substantially reflecting the large regional differences in real incomes.

A large part of the urban-rural differences in real terms arises from non-food consumption. This is significant considering that the non-food price index in this paper may have overstated the true urban-rural price differences. In spite of a markedly higher non-food/food relative price in urban areas compared to rural zones, urban dwellers consume relatively more non-food items than food compared to the rural people. The higher urban income and the higher income elasticity for non-food items relative to food are probably the main reasons. But the question also relates to why urban dwellers with equal or higher real incomes, in some cases, consume less food and more non-food than their rural counterparts. Part of the explanation may lie in quality differences of the items consumed. Urban consumption of certain non-food categories which are simply not available in rural areas may be another part of the explanation.

Between urban and rural locations within regions, a major part of differences in well-being arises from differences in the consumption of non-food categories. This result points to large urban/rural disparities within these regions in the availability of public goods and services and the like, rather than in nutritional levels. But across regions, differentials in mean food consumption are by no means insignificant, and serious nutritional inadequacies are brought out in the case of some.

Various measures of poverty confirm the types of disparities within Brazil noted thus far. A conservative definition of poverty at the national aggregate level indicates that if a 5% increase in annual national income above the levels existing in 1974/75 were entirely directed towards the poor, everyone would have been at or above the poverty line. The more interesting outcome of the poverty measures undoubtedly points out that considerably more poverty exists in the nation's rural areas than in urban areas. For instance, a poverty index for the nation's rural areas is approximately 20% higher than the national average, while that of the metropolitan areas is roughly 50% below national averages. Compared to such urban-rural differences, however, some regional differences, particularly between the Northeast and the Southeast, are more striking. The sharpest contrast is provided by a comparison of the state of Sao Paulo with the Northeast region. While a

Table I.1: SELECTED WELFARE INDICATORS - BRAZIL VS REST OF THE WORLD

Country Classification	Population (million) (1978)	Population Density (No/km²) (1978)	GNP Per Capita US$ (1978)	GNP Per Capita Annual Average Rate (%) (1960-78)	Urban Population (% of total) (1980)	Population Per Doctor (1977)	% Calorie Requirement Achieved (1977)	% Population With Potable Water (1975)	Adult Literacy Rate (%) (1975)	Life Expectancy at Birth (1978)
Brazil	119.5	14.0	1,570	4.9	65	1,700	107	77	76	62
Low Income	1,293.9	49.1	200	1.6	21	9,900	91	28	38	50
Bangladesh	84.7	588.1	90	-0.4	11	9,260	78	53	26	47
India	643.9	195.8	180	1.4	22	3,620	91	33	36	51
Tanzania	16.9	17.8	230	2.7	12	15,450	89	39	66	51
Indonesia	136.0	67.0	360	4.1	20	14,580	105	12	62	47
Middle Income	872.8	26.4	1,250	3.7	51	4,310	108	60	71	61
Peru	16.8	13.0	740	2.0	67	1,560	97	47	72	56
Nicaragua	2.5	19.2	840	2.3	53	1,670	109	70	57	55
Colombia	25.6	22.4	850	3.0	70	1,970	102	64	81	62
Argentina	26.4	9.5	1,910	2.6	82	530	126	66	94	71
Yugoslavia	22.0	85.9	2,380	5.4	42	760	136	-	85	69
Industrialized	667.8	21.9	8,070	3.7	77	630	131	-	99	74
UK	55.8	228.6	5,030	2.1	91	750	132	-	99	73
Japan	114.9	308.8	7,280	7.6	78	850	126	-	99	76
West Germany	61.3	246.1	9,580	3.3	85	490	127	-	99	72
USA	221.9	23.6	9,590	2.4	73	580	135	-	99	73
Petroleum Exporters	60.1	9.9	3,340	7.1	58	1,830	115	58	50	53
Iraq	12.2	28.0	1,860	4.1	72	2,230	89	62	-	55
Saudi Arabia	8.2	3.8	7,690	9.7	67	1,690	88	64	-	53
Centrally Planned	1,352.4	38.8	1,190	4.0	36	390	114	-	-	70
China	952.2	99.2	230	3.7	25	-	105	-	-	70
USSR	261.0	11.6	3,700	4.3	65	300	135	-	99	70

Source: World Bank, World Development Report, Annex - World Development Indicators: Tables 1, 20, 21, 22 and 23.

Table I.2: DEMOGRAPHIC AND SOCIO-ECONOMIC INDICATORS - BRAZIL BY REGIONS /a

Regions	Population Growth Rate (%) (1979)	Population Density (No/km^2) (1975)	Urban Population (% total) (1980)	% Employed Working Less Than 39 Hours/Week (1978)	% Pop. Over 10 Years With Income Less Than Two Minimum Wages (1978)	% Population With 7-14 Years Enrolled in School (1978)	Adult Literacy Rate (1970)	Cars Per 1,000 People (1970)
Region I	2.9	240.17	93.2	13.47	32.51	78.62	77.4	28.9
Region II	3.1	83.44	91.9	9.25	32.55	81.62	85.3	34.8
Region III	3.1	34.26	49.0	15.04	35.71	76.02	70.1	20.2
Region IV	1.8	22.73	64.2	12.36	38.88	78.47	59.0	11.9
Region V	2.5	20.80	47.4	19.60	42.78	52.48	38.0	5.4
Region VI	-	132.26	-	10.01	27.61	80.17	75.4	32.4
Region VII	3.7 /b	1.80	52.7 /b	14.51	38.35	70.70	54.6	7.2
BRAZIL	2.8	12.59	63.5	14.09 /c	37.47 /c	70.11 /c	55.9	16.6

/a See Annex Table 1 for definition of regions.
/b Includes Region VI.
/c Approximated average using population weights of the regions.

Source: IBGE, 1978 "Anuario Estatistico", Chapters 5, 9, 17; IBGE, 1970, "Censos Demograficos Estaduais", Table 10.

Table I.3: SELECTED HEALTH AND WELFARE INDICATORS - BRAZIL BY REGIONS

Regions	Population Per Doctor (1974)	Population Per Hospital Bed (1977)	Number of Health Centers per 1000 People (1974)	% Population Without Piped Water (1970)	% Residents With Internal Sewerage (1979)	% Residents With Access to General Sewerage (1979)	% Residents With Electricity (1979)	Calorie Deficit/a (%)
Region I	769.9	158.6	0.0705	55.4	76.83	47.83	89.35	- 7.9
Region II	1,101.8	185.7	0.0235	41.4	75.01	51.21	89.98	+ 4.7
Region III	1,987.8	235.5	0.0246	74.7	42.87	11.84	56.25	+ 4.5
Region IV	2,017.0	252.1	0.0328	69.0	48.32	29.27	54.87	+ 4.5
Region V	2,996.0	453.0	0.0214	87.6	20.68	3.70	34.29	-12.6
Region VI	737.7	215.8	0.0152	34.2	74.87	51.86	94.85	-12.1
Region VII	3,265.0	306.9	0.0046	78.0	46.99	12.76	69.99	-15.2
BRAZIL	1,707.7	254.2	0.0238/b	67.2	46.96/b	23.57/b	60.24/b	- 3.1/b

/a (-) indicates deficit and (+) surplus.
/b Approximated average using population weights of the regions.

Source: IPE, INAN: "Avaliacao Global do Programa de Nutricao-BRASIL/BIRD, 1980".

poverty index for Sao Paulo state is roughly 2 1/2 times below the national average, that for the Northeast is 1 2/3 as high as this average.

II. Regional and Urban-Rural Variations in Living Costs

Large spatial differences in the cost of living exist within Brazil. Price differences are experienced across regions and between urban and rural areas. Cost variations for non-food categories are clearly greater than for food items, although the magnitude of these differences has yet to be fully and accurately quantified.

Several studies (see below) have brought out differences in food prices. Such work has been facilitated by the availability of data on food expenditures and quantities consumed for major regions and areas 1/. Although food items vary in quality across locations, fairly reliable price comparisons have been possible on the basis of available data. Cost differences estimates for non-food categories, on the other hand, have been hard to come by. Well-known problems in comparing these items across places have stood in the way of developing estimates. FIBGE estimates cost of living indices for major cities based on a basket of food and non-food items 2/. While these are useful in indicating price changes over

---

1/ See FIBGE [13], [14], [15], FGV [9], [10], FIPE [11].

2/ Other institutes prepare independent estimates for individual cities, as for example FIPE [11] for Sao Paulo.

time, their reliability for comparing prices spatially is limited by tremendous differences in the baskets of non-food items considered.

In a recent World Bank study [20], comparisons were made of the cost of meeting minimum calorie requirements across Brazil. Various food baskets were compared using the ENDEF data for 1974/75 [12], [13] 1/ and in all cases, costs varied substantially. For instance, the cost of the diet of a typical (i.e. average) family that just meets the minimum requirements in metropolitan Sao Paulo exceeds that in the state's rural areas by 2.1 times and that in the rural areas of the Northeast region by 2.7 times. Food cost differences within the Northeast have been reported by Prado and Macedo [32]. Using the ENDEF data for 1974/75, the cost of an "average" basket in the city of Salvador was estimated to be about 25% more than in the rural areas.

Williamson [45] has calculated price differences among 22 of the ENDEF regions and areas for major food sub-groups. Inter-city price differences have been estimated by Malard Meyer [26], also using the ENDEF data. Hicks and Vetter [16] have measured the costs of "poverty line food baskets" for various Brazilian cities.

Some measures of non-food cost variations for urban areas have been made by Medeiros [27] using data provided by FIBGE. These measures

---

1/ Apart from these published data, some unpublished information for the prices applicable to the people at the 20th percentile of the expenditure distribution was also used.

are essentially expenditure differences for people within fairly small income ranges (and thus considered comparable). For these people, all expenditure differences were assumed to be price differences. Housing cost in metropolitan Rio de Janeiro was estimated to be 2.2 times that in non-metropolitan areas in the Northeast, and 2 times that in non-metropolitan urban areas in the Southeast.

For overall cost of living differences, some approximations were made by Pfeffermann and Webb [31]. Between metropolitan and other urban areas, differences of 20% were indicated; between metropolitan and rural areas diffferences of 30% were indicated.

Estimates of cost of living differentials are important in this paper. They make expenditure data comparable across locations, and allow measurement of spatial differences in the incidence of poverty. In the rest of this section, we develop cost of living measures and discuss results contained in Tables II.1 and Annex Table 5.

We use the ENDEF data to estimate food, non-food and overall price indices for the seven major regions (see previous section), and metropolitan, non-metropolitan urban and rural areas within those regions, as well as for the country as a whole. A first measure compares people at the mean. The ENDEF data reveal, however, that in different places, people at the mean belong to quite different expenditure classes. Consequently, price indices at the mean may be comparing the cost of baskets of goods that are quite different qualitatively. To minimize this problem, a second measure attempts to compare people at the 40th percentile of the expenditure distribution. The choice of the 40th percentile enables us to compare the relatively poorer people, while avoiding major inconsistencies in the data found at lower percentiles. Placing people at the 40th percentile, however, is not straightforward since available expenditure data distribute people within discrete expenditure classes whose end points sometimes differ significantly from the 40th percentile. We have tried to circumvent this problem by assuming a normal expenditure distribution in the neighborhood of the 40th percentile, thus approximating expenditure for the 40th percentile.

Published ENDEF data give expenditure distribution for families. Using information on family sizes for expenditure classes, we have constructed per capita expenditure distribution. If family sizes vary widely across expenditure classes, this procedure can be misleading. In the case of some rural areas this has been so. In the majority of the other cases, however, in the neighborhood of the 40th percentile, family sizes do not vary enough to cause problems.

A. Food Prices

It has been possible to calculate the prices of over 120 individual food items for the various regions and areas in 1974/75 on the basis of the ENDEF data on family expenditures and quantities consumed 1/. There exist alternative ways of weighting these prices across items and

---

1/ Prices of items consumed at restaurants have been omitted.

across locations to obtain spatial price indices for food. For a first set of estimates, the approach adopted in this paper is to obtain the spatial price differences of a basket of all food items in their national average proportions. This corresponds to a Laspeyres price index 1/.

First, a price index for each of the food items has been calculated 2/. The base for this index is the national price which has been obtained by weighting each location's price by the location's quantity weight in the national total. These price indices have then been weighted across the various items using their respective expenditure shares at the national level. The resulting price index for any location reflects the difference in that location from the national price (assumed to be 100) of a nationally consumed average basket of food.

Annex Tables 3 and 5 set out the price indices for ten major sub-groups of food items and for a composite food bundle. Significant

---

1/ I.e.
$$P_j = \frac{\sum_{i=1}^{n} X_{im} P_{ij}}{\sum_{i=1}^{n} X_{im} P_{im}}, \text{ or,}$$

$$\sum_{i=1}^{n} \left(\frac{P_{ij}}{P_{im}}\right) \frac{X_{im} P_{im}}{\sum_i X_{im} P_{im}}$$

where P and X are prices and quantities respectively for commodity i going from 1 to n in any location j compared to a national average location m.

2/ To see this, one may divide expenditure estimates in [13] by the corresponding quantity estimates in [12] for any item.

price differences are indicated. Comparing metropolitan Sao Paulo, the largest urban center, with adjacent rural areas (i.e. in Region II), for instance, an urban-rural price difference of 14% is observed. Comparing metropolitan Sao Paulo with the even more rural situation of the Northeast (i.e. in Region V), a price difference of 35% is noted.

Regional difference is a part of the latter result. The average price in Sao Paulo state (i.e. Region II) is 16% higher than in the Northeast, as summarized in Table II.1 below. Of the first five regions, the first two containing, respectively, Rio de Janeiro and Sao Paulo, have higher food prices than Regions III, IV and V. It should be noted in comparing these with the remaining two that Region VI is all urban (Brasilia), and that rural areas are excluded from Region VII.

The results provide locational price differences of a nationally consumed average basket of food items. A limitation of this approach, however, lies in its use of national expenditure weights rather than of location-specific ones. An alternative method would be to express at national prices the cost of baskets of food consumed in each place. In this procedure, corresponding to Paasche's price index, expenditure weights of individual locations rather than the national averages would be made use of [1]. Clearly, least-cost options available in individual locations should be reflected. This would be best done by considering

---

[1] I.e. $P_j = \sum_{i=1}^{n} \left(\frac{P_{im}}{P_{ij}}\right) \frac{X_{ij} P_{ij}}{\Sigma_i X_{ij} P_{ij}}$

price differences of low-cost location-specific food baskets rather than a nationwide average basket. On the other hand, in indicating overall spatial differences in food prices, it may be logical to first compare one national composite food basket.

In this paper, we make use of the Laspeyres index to indicate overall spatial price differences of food and to yield regional comparisons of overall food consumption. In the construction of poverty levels, on the other hand, the cost is compared between baskets of food, maintaining their location-specific proportions. One price index based on a location-specific consumption pattern is given in the second column of Annex Table 5 and Table II.1. This index, constructed from data in the World Bank study [20], essentially shows the price differences of a food basket consumed by people at the 20th percentile of the expenditure distribution, maintaining each location's consumption pattern at that income range. The large urban-rural price differences according to this index reflect the ability of the poor in rural areas to meet minimum nutritional needs at relatively low costs, if their own actual consumption patterns were maintained.

Both the price indices show that food prices increase, going from rural to urban areas and from the more rural to the more urbanized regions. Regions I and II, as well as VI, where the percentage of urban population is high (see Annex Table 2), consistently show a price level well above the national average. Regions IV and V (Espirito Santo and

Minas Gerais), as well as Region III (the South), are less urbanized and also face below national average prices.

The above price index based on the consumption pattern of the 20th percentile is the basis for one of the poverty measures presented later in this paper (Annex Table 17, Column 3). In the use of a price index to estimate poverty levels, as opposed to deflating incomes, an issue is raised relating to the weighting of costs across locations to obtain a national average. In the case of Laspeyres' or Paasche's price indices, described earlier, weighting by quantities consumed of individual items and by expenditures across items are appropriate. For use in estimating the number of poor, or for measuring incomes needed to eliminate poverty, the weighting of costs or prices must take into account the number of people affected by the relevant costs or prices.

To take an example, if 80% of the national population who live in location 1 face P_1 and 20% in location 2 face P_2 for a poverty basket of food, the national average income needed to obtain one poverty basket would be the average of P_1 and P_2 weighted by the respective population weights, .8 and .2. Weighting by the quantities consumed in the two locations would be inappropriate. Thus, in the section on poverty measures, regional average and national average poverty levels are constructed by weighting average location-specific poverty lines, using population weights.

B. Non-Food Prices

The ENDEF data for non-food do not permit derivation of price indices as in the case of food because no estimates of the quantities consumed are given. No other independent estimates of non-food prices are available for the ENDEF regions and areas, even for the major items. We have, therefore, tried to approximate spatial price ratios from available data on expenditure differentials.

A given expenditure difference between two locations may be in extreme cases entirely due to a price difference or to a quantity difference. We have assumed that in reality only part of the difference is due to a price difference, the rest being due to a quantity difference 1/. The non-food quantity difference is postulated to arise, on the one hand, because money incomes (total expenditures) vary, and on the other, because non-food prices vary. Differences in incomes along with an income elasticity of demand, and difference in prices along with a price elasticity of demand, together explain the non-food quantity variation. To obtain a price ratio, with the national average as a base, we write the known expenditure ratio between any location j and a hypothetical national average (calculated) m as equal to the ratio between price in j and the price in m (of 100) times the quantity ratio. The latter quantity ratio

---

1/ In the estimation of poverty lines, we provide lower and upper bound estimates that would result if, respectively, all expenditure differences are assumed to be due to quantity differences, and due to price differences. See Section V.D.

is related to the income and price differences between j and m and the income and price elasticities at m. This helps us to solve for the price in j as a proportion of the price in m of 100.

The above approach identifies the change in quantity consumed by a hypothetical person who experiences a change in income and price in going from m to j, leaving the remaining difference as the price variation. The estimated quantity change is dictated by the elasticities measured in the hypothetical average location (i.e., using data for all locations). This method will not fully identify differences in the quantity consumed in a particular place that arise due to location-specific needs. The procedure used, for instance, will not fully reflect that part of the urban people's higher consumption arising purely from their being city dwellers--for example, the larger quantities consumed of transportation, clothing, and safety devices. Such quantity differences, beyond those in the "average" location, will instead become part of the price differences. This feature of our method is reasonable insofar as this type of quantity differences does not enhance welfare (e.g., urban dwellers are not better off because they travel more). If, on the contrary, it contributes to welfare, the price index as calculated in this paper for urban areas will be biased upwards.

To apply this method, price and income elasticities of demand for non-food could not be calculated, since no data on quantities of non-food consumed were available. It has been possible, however, to use estimated elasticities for food along with average budget shares of food and non-food to derive non-food elasticities, applying the Slutsky equations [42]. This above procedure was outlined, and an equation for the non-food price index applied for the case of Peru in an earlier paper [43].

The main improvement in this study is that we develop estimates restricting the comparison to the 40th percentile of the nominal expenditure distribution, in addition to the comparison at the mean as before. We believe that comparisons at the 40th percentile reduce the quality differences inherent at the mean. The resultant price differences, therefore, represent more accurately the difference in the cost of a comparable basket.

To separate out the quantity variation from the expenditure change across locations at the 40th percentile, we have calculated income and price elasticities of demand for food at that income range using the ENDEF data [38]. These are respectively 0.86 and -1.2. To be used for transforming these food elasticities into non-food elasticities, national average budget shares of food and non-food were calculated to be respectively 0.4 and 0.6. For comparison, calculations have also been made for the mean, in which case the demand elasticities of income and price for food used were respectively 0.54 and -0.38 1/.

1/ For comparison with other countries, see [24], [28].

The use of national budget shares and national elasticities is analogous to the use of national weights to obtain regional prices applying Laspeyres indices in the case of food 1/. Budget shares are clearly non-uniform across regions (Annex Table 10), and the significant urban-rural differences in price and income elasticities are bound to exist. To provide an idea of the sensitivity of the results to varying budget shares and elasticities, we tried a number of alternative estimates. It turned out that in the application of the Slutsky equations, such variations did not affect results significantly.

Income and price elasticities of demand at the 40th percentile have been calculated using only data on monetary expenditure. These elasticities indicate changes in the quantities purchased in the market as a result of changes in money income and price. The resultant price index reflects cost variation across locations of buying non-food categories in the market. If non-monetary items were correctly and fully imputed in the ENDEF data, their inclusion in the elasticity calculation should not alter the above price index--except to the extent that the composition of items may change with the inclusion of non-monetary expenditure items.

The reason why only monetary expenditure items have been used in the above was that several inconsistencies were found in the data for the 40th percentile, particularly for rural areas when non-monetary components

---

1/ The alternative, analogous to Paasche's, would be to compare the national average with each location as a base.

were included. For the mean, however, this problem was much less serious except in a few rural areas. Therefore, we were able to utilize the total expenditure data (i.e. monetary plus non-monetary) for this case.

Annex Table 5 provides the estimated price indices for the mean and the 40th percentile. The wide price fluctuation at the mean (Col. II, A) are reduced at the 40th percentile (Col. II, B). Comparing the same range in the expenditure distribution, much of the heterogeneity of the basket and quality of goods compared are likely to be reduced, thus giving a smaller price divergence. It appears that the kinds of non-food items consumed at the mean across Brazil vary widely, causing the large apparent price variations in Col. II, A.

While the quality problem is by no means removed, a better comparison of the price of a non-food basket is possible at the 40th percentile in Col. II, B. Prices vary systematically, exceeding 100 in the urban and relatively more urbanized regions, and falling below 100 in the more rural locations. There is almost a one-to-one correspondence between the price index and the degree of urbanization, going from metropolitan Sao Paulo, Brasilia and metropolitan Rio de Janeiro to the rural areas of Espirito Santo and Minas Gerais and the Northeast. The non-food price in metropolitan Sao Paulo is 165% higher than rural areas in Region II. Table II.1 summarizes the non-food price variation among the major regions and areas. A regional difference of 80% is recorded between Region II and Region IV. Between the metropolitan areas and other urban areas in the country as a whole, a price difference of 53% is estimated.

Considering the limitations of the non-food price estimates presented above, we tried to directly assemble price estimates for major non-food categories. Work is underway at FIBGE in constructing price indices for "comparable" housing and other major non-food categories. It has not been possible to incorporate results of this work in this paper. Presented are some independent calculations of housing price differentials among several Brazilian cities.

The 1970 Demographic Census provides information on rents paid by nine different rent groups in 126 urban municipalities located in the states of Rio de Janeiro, Sao Paulo, Minas Gerais, Espirito Santo, Parana, Santa Catarina, Rio Grande de Sul and Goias, and Brasilia. For metropolitan areas within these states, several municipalities were aggregated. It was possible to separate out the rent paid for four-room urban houses serviced by water and sewer networks within these rent groups. From this information, median rents were calculated for what may _roughly_ be considered comparable housing in each of the municipalities. The results for the metropolitan areas and some other urban areas are presented in Annex Table 4. Results for selected metropolitan areas are given below.

Median Rents for Comparable Housing - 1970

	Price Index
Rio de Janeiro	137
Sao Paulo	126
Porto Alegre	122
Curitiba	105
Belo Horizonte	105
Brasilia	146
Average /a	100

/a Average for 126 municipalities; see Annex Table 4.

C. Overall Prices

The overall price is a weighted average of the food and non-food prices, the weights being the relative importance of these items in total expenditure. Overall prices have been calculated using the non-food index for the 40th percentile, and alternatively the food price index at the mean and for the low-cost diet. The full range of likely price variation within Brazil is shown based on these indices in Annex Table 5, which is summarized in Table II.1. The more affluent and urbanized locations clearly display higher price levels. At the mean, metropolitan Sao Paulo's prices are roughly twice those in the state's rural areas and about 1.25 times those in the rural areas of Regions III and IV. Region II's prices are roughly 50% higher than in Regions III and IV. Compared to the national average, the metropolitan areas' prices for lower income groups are about 50% higher, while the rural areas' prices are probably about 25% lower 1/. The non-metropolitan urban areas' prices correspond roughly to the national average.

III. Spatial Inequality of Income

Wide disparities in incomes in Brazil have been documented 2/. According to data presented in the World Development Report [46], Brazil's

---

1/ Urban-rural comparisons are approximations for the Northeast and the nation as a whole due to data problems in rural Northeast. See Table III.2.

2/ See [17], [21], [22], [23], [25], [31], [32].

Table II.1: ESTIMATED FOOD, NON-FOOD AND OVERALL PRICE INDICES FOR REGIONS AND AREAS: BRAZIL (1974/75)

	I. Food		II Non-Food	III. Overall	
	A. National Average Basket /a	B. Location Specific Basket of 20th Perc.	Based on 40th Perc. Expenditure	A. National Average Food and Non-Food	B. Low Cost 20th Perc. Food and Non-Food
I. Regions					
Region I	111	126	175	151	162
Region II	116	123	148	138	141
Region III	96	95*	94	95	94
Region IV	96	82	87	90	85
Region V	100	83	n.a.	n.a.	n.a.
Region VI	121	140	156	146	152
Region VII	118	78	110	113	100
II. Areas					
Metropolitan	n.a.	131	161	n.a.	154
Other Urban	n.a.	93	105	n.a.	100
Rural	n.a.	78*	n.a.	n.a.	n.a.
III. National Average	100	100	100	100	100

n.a. - Not available, due to inconsistencies in the data. See Table III.1.
* - An exceptionally large non-monetary component for rural areas makes this price index questionable. See Table III.2.
/a Using national weights.

Source: Annex Table 5.

income distribution in 1972 was more skewed than in most other countries for which comparable data were available. The lowest 20% of households shared only 2% of total household income while the top 10% gained 51%. There has been much debate whether this situation has worsened in recent years or not. Pfeffermann and Webb [31] bring out salient issues of this debate.

Whether income distribution has been worsening or not, there is little doubt that existing disparities are large. A major support for this notion is the extent of visible backwardness of certain regions and areas in relation to the rest of the country. The poverty found in the Northeast, for instance, is in sharp contrast to the standard of living in the Southeast. In this section we focus on the extent of spatial inequality of income, setting aside issues of interpersonal income distribution and its change over time.

We draw on the results of the ENDEF survey to compare expenditure levels across locations. Expenditure measures usually achieve better coverage of total income than alternative income estimates from employment surveys, for instance. ENDEF's expenditure estimates include measures for non-monetary income as well. Three levels of expenditure include annual expenses on food, clothing, housing, health, personal care, transport, education and others. A second measure includes, in addition, taxes and contribution. Global expenditure, a third measure, includes all other acquisitions as well. The unit for all these measurements is the family. The family sizes are also given so that per capita estimates can be made.

The survey procedure and a detailed explanation of definitions and concepts used can be found in FIBGE [13].

A. Nominal Expenditures

If cost of living differences were negligible, nominal expenditures would reflect real income differences. But as shown in Section 2, prices vary widely, and therefore nominal expenditures are inaccurate measures of the real differences. Nevertheless, we first examine nominal magnitudes, in part simply to indicate how income variations are narrowed when nominal magnitudes are deflated by price indices.

Annex Tables 6 and 7 present data compiled from ENDEF for various types of expenditures by locations. Annex Table 8 and Table III.1 below give these data in the form of indices (with the national average as a base) to highlight the differences. These data reflect spatial divergencies in the average nominal incomes. The wealthiest regions in nominal terms are I, II and VI; their average incomes are generally 50% above the national average. Regions IV and V are worst off with incomes roughly 20% to 50%, respectively, below the national average. Incomes of Regions III and VII roughly correspond to the national average.

The relative positions of Regions I, II and VI are largely due to the income levels of their metropolitan areas -- Rio de Janeiro, Sao Paulo and Brasilia. Nominal incomes in all metropolitan areas -- except Fortaleza and Recife in Region V -- are well above the national average. Rural areas, on the other hand, fall well below the average. For the nation as a whole, metropolitan areas have roughly twice the national average and rural areas less than half. The non-metropolitan urban areas' income roughly corresponds to the national average.

The variations are not uniform across types of expenditures. Monetary expenditures always show greater variations. Clearly non-monetary components are more important in the rural areas and the more rural regions. The comparative positions of these locations are improved with the inclusion of non-monetary items (compare Columns 1 and 2 in Table III.1). Similarly the rural locations fare better when current expenditures are compared rather than global. Acquisitions of a durable nature are proportionately more important in the urban areas and the more urban regions. Consumption expenditure improves the comparative position of the rural locations further, indicating that taxes and contributions are relatively less important in these places.

In general, the variance of non-food expenditure, whether consumption, current or global, or whether monetary or non-monetary, is far greater than of food. In Annex Table 7, the current expenses for non-food of the metropolitan areas exceeds that of the other urban areas by 2.2 times, and the rural areas by 5.7 times. In the case of food, on the other hand, the metropolitan "other urban" divergence falls to 1.4 and the metropolitan-rural to 1.7 (see Annex Tables 9 and 10).

Annex Table 11 shows the percentage distribution of major consumption items in total current expenditure. Locations that are poorer in terms of nominal income spend a greater proportion on food. Non-food items, like housing and transport, explain the bulk of higher expenses in the higher income locations.

Solorzano [38] has also estimated nominal expenditures of people belonging to the 40th percentile of the expenditure distribution in each place from ENDEF. A smooth continuous distribution of expenditure was assumed in the neighborhood of the 40th percentile, permitting the approximation of the expenditure of someone at that percentile that falls between two discrete given intervals. Admittedly tentative, these estimates enable us to compare people who belong to the same relative position in the distribution in each place. The people compared also constitute a lower income group than in the comparison of the mean.

Table III.3 summarizes the main urban and regional comparisons at the 40th percentile. The broad differences observed at the mean in nominal expenditures hold. It is noteworthy, however, that overall differences are narrowed at the 40th percentile in comparison with the mean 1/. If this were so at various percentiles below the mean, it would imply a better income distribution in the more rural locations. But this certainly cannot be concluded on the basis of the relative positions of

---

1/ Compare Tables III.2 and III.3.

people at a single point. The 40th percentile is a high point in the income distribution of the poor. It is possible that a larger concentration of the poor below this point exists in the more rural locations, giving them actually a worse overall income distribution than the urban locations. It will be indicated in Section V that although the ENDEF data point to a better income distribution in the rural areas, the evidence is not conclusive.

B. Real Expenditures

Division of nominal expenditures on food and non-food by their respective price indices yields real expenditures. The detailed results for the mean are given in Annex Table 12. Also given in these tables are the totals of the nominal and real magnitudes of the two categories. These estimates show how spatial divergencies narrow when nominal figures are deflated by price indices. The results for the major regions and areas for the mean are summarized in Table III.2.

1. Food Consumption

Nominal expenses vary less in the case of food than non-food. Yet the more urban locations generally display significantly higher nominal food expenditures. Deflation by the food price index changes this result. As Tables III.2 and III.3 show, urban-rural differences are drastically reduced, and in some cases, reversed. However, considerable regional differences persist.

The narrowing of estimated food consumption is greater in the case of total expenditure than if monetary expenditure alone were used (not shown). The reason is that the rural locations have far greater non-monetary components whose urban-rural price differences are larger than for monetary items. Consequently, the use of price indices for total expenses (i.e. monetary, plus non-monetary) raises real expenses of the more rural locations relative to urban ones, more than in the use of price indices based only on monetary expenses. The real total expenses on food are thus generally more uniform across space.

Urban-rural gaps narrow more at the 40th percentile than at the mean in most cases (Solorzano [38], Table 12). The reason of course is that the food price index at the 40th percentile has a greater urban-rural spread than at the mean (Annex Table 5). The reason, suggested in Section II, was that in comparing a relatively lower income group (i.e., people at the 40th percentile), relatively more purchase of inexpensive items is allowed for in the rural than in the urban areas.

To show the broad differences in food consumption within Brazil, we refer to Tables III.2 and III.3. The former table for the mean compares an "average" individual in each place; the latter for the 40th percentile utilizes the price index for a more homogeneous basket in comparing people at the same relative positions in the income scale. In real terms regional differences in food consumption are reduced at the mean and the 40th percentile. Although the gap in food intake, if represented by real rather than nominal consumption, is considerably narrowed one can observe significant disparities as related to income differences among regions. The sharpest contrast is between the Northeast and the rest of the country. Food consumption is the lowest in this former region, which also has the lowest income levels.

The large urban-rural differences in nominal terms are also sharply reduced when comparisons are made in real terms. Nevertheless, at the mean, urban areas in general show greater food intake. When the situation of lower income groups at the 40th percentile is considered, however, the position of the rural people improves even further relative to the urban group. Solorzano [38] suggests that in some instances rural consumption of food in real terms might be even higher than that in the metropolitan areas.

The possibility of better food intake in some rural areas is supported in Section IV where comparisons are made of the percentages of nutritional requirements achieved -- although judgments are made based only on caloric intake across the country. It is shown that while the more rural areas among the high income regions -- viz. Regions II and III, along with the moderately wealthy but largely rural Region IV -- achieve the highest intake of calories absolutely and relative to requirements, the other high income regions, I and VI, which are the most urbanized (see Annex Table 1) perform worse. The nation's poorest region, the Northeast, and particularly its metropolitan areas, remain worst off.

2. Non-Food Consumption

Nominal expenses on non-food items vary far more than on food. The non-food price index also had a larger spread than the food price index. Consequently, real expense differences are brought down more in the case of non-food than food. Nevertheless, larger spatial divergencies remain in non-food consumption than in food.

Unlike the case of food, price indices for non-food are based on only one type of expenditure -- total non-food expenses for the mean and only monetary non-food expenses for the 40th percentile (see Section II). Although separate indices were calculated for the mean and the 40th percentile, it was pointed out that substantial quality variations of non-food items at the mean might render the index at the mean unrepresentative. Solorzano [38] presents real expenses based on both types of price indices, and Tables III.2 and III.3 summarize the main results. A full comparison of regions and areas on the basis of the 40th percentile, in particular, has not been possible due to inconsistencies in the data for certain rural areas.

The more urbanized regions and the urban areas achieve a much higher consumption of non-food categories than the rest of the country. This is so at the mean and comparing the 40th percentile. People in regions I, II and VI, with the largest metropolitan centers (Rio, Sao Paulo and Brasilia, respectively) consume, on the average, more non-food items than the national average 1/. The moderately urbanized Region III also consumes a little over the average, while the largely rural Northeast (Region V) and Region IV fall below the average. The Northeast consumes less than half of Regions I, II and VI.

Non-food consumption thus appears to vary positively with not only income but also the degree of urbanization. This is clearly brought out in the comparison of areas. Contrary to the case of food, non-food consumption in the metropolitan areas exceeds that in the urban areas significantly at the 40th percentile. The gap is 18%.

3. Total Consumption

Summing the food and non-food categories, we obtain total consumption. In contrast to nominal expenditures, this resulting measure

---

1/ This is not very precise because the national average in this case had to be calculated excluding rural Northeast.

of consumption (real) displays smaller spatial variance. The major part of the remaining differences -- particularly if lower income groups are compared -- arises from disparities in non-food consumption.

At the 40th percentile the overall metropolitan-urban-rural variation is brought down considerably, but is by no means eliminated. An estimated excess of metropolitan consumption over other urban areas of 2% and over rural areas of 27% remains even when comparing people belonging to the same position in expenditure distributions. At the mean, larger urban-rural differences persist.

Table III.1: SPATIAL DIFFERENCES IN NOMINAL EXPENDITURES
(ANNUAL PER CAPITA) - BRAZIL (1974/75)
Indices: Base-National Average = 100

	Global Monetary	Global Monetary and Non-Mon.	Current Monetary	Current Monetary and Non-Mon.	Consumption Monetary	Consumption Monetary and Non-Mon.
Regions						
Region I	183	177	192	182	187	207
Region II	155	150	144	140	142	139
Region III	99	102	94	99	95	100
Region IV	81	83	80	83	81	84
Region V	44	46	50	54	52	53
Region VI	162	164	173	171	169	169
Region VII	106	106	113	112	115	113
Areas						
Metropolitan	200	192	193	184	189	180
Other Urban	98	96	100	96	101	97
Rural	36	44	39	50	41	51

Source: Annex Table 8.

Table III.2: ESTIMATED ANNUAL PER CAPITA CURRENT EXPENDITURE (TOTAL) a/
NOMINAL AND REAL b/ AT THE MEAN FOR REGIONS AND AREAS
BRAZIL (1974/75)
(Cruzeiros, 1974)

	Food Nominal	Food Real	Non-Food Nominal	Non-Food Real	Total Nominal	Total Real
Regions						
Region I c/	1,895	1,707	5,100	2,914	6,995	4,621
	(2,132)	(1,921)	(5,737)	(3,278)	(7,869)	(5,199)
Region II	1,674	1,443	4,419	2,985	6,093	4,428
Region III	1,542	1,606	2,746	2,921	4,288	4,527
Region IV	1,323	1,378	2,285	2,626	3,609	4,004
Region V	1,029	1,029	1,234	(1,260)*	2,357	(2,289)*
Region VI	1,711	1,414	5,707	3,658	7,418	5,072
Region VII d/	1,681	1,425	3,163	2,875	4,844	4,300
Selected Cities						
Porto Alegre	2,093	1,937	6,207	3,928	8,300	5,765
Sao Paulo	2,228	1,797	7,399	3,574	9,627	5,371
Rio de Janeiro	2,219	1,930	6,381	3,289	8,601	5,219
Brasilia	1,711	1,414	5,707	?	7,418	5,072
Salvador	1,599	1,333	4,857	3,652	6,456	4,885
National Average	1,441	1,441	2,880	2,880	4,321	4,321

a/ I.e., monetary plus non-monetary.
b/ I.e., dividing nominal by a price index with its base = national average price.
c/ There is some ambiguity about the appropriate average family size to be used for this region, giving two alternative per capita estimates, the first assuming average family size of 4.5, and the second 4.
d/ Excludes rural areas.

* The construction of non-food price index using total (i.e., monetary plus non-monetary) non-food expenditure for the rural Northeast brought out inconsistencies. An approximation using monetary expenses alone was made, giving these tentative results.

Source: Annex Table 12.

Table III.3: ESTIMATED ANNUAL PER CAPITA CURRENT EXPENDITURE (TOTAL) a/
NOMINAL AND REAL b/ AT THE 40TH PERCENTILE FOR REGIONS AND AREAS
BRAZIL (1974/75)
(Cruzeiros, 1974)

	Food Nominal	Food Real	Non-Food Nominal	Non-Food Real	Total Nominal	Total Real
Regions						
Region I	1,800	1,428	2,501	1,429	4,301	2,857
Region II	1,821	1,480	2,680	1,811	4,501	3,291
Region III	1,524	(1,604)*	1,388	1,476	2,912	(3,080)
Region IV	1,064	1,297	973	1,118	2,037	2,415
Region V	802	966	549	(677)**	1,351	(1,643)
Region VI c/	1,424	1,017	2,499	1,601	3,923	2,618
Region VII d/	1,345	1,724	1,319	1,242	2,664	2,966
Areas						
Metropolitan	1,589	1,213	2,580	1,602	4,169	2,815
Other Areas	1,302	1,400	1,420	1,352	2,722	2,752
Rural	1,040	(1,333)*	590	(880)**	1,630	(2,213)

a/ I.e., monetary plus non-monetary.
b/ I.e., dividing nominal by a price index with its base = national average price.
c/ Excludes rural areas.

* An exceptionally large non-monetary component in Region III's rural areas appears to render the rural price index, and hence real expense, for the rural areas for this region questionable. An approximation for the price using monetary expenses alone was made with these resulting real expense estimates.

** The non-food price index at the 40th percentile for Rural Northeast could not be calculated. An approximation from mean monetary differences was made, giving these real expenditure estimates.

Source: Solorzano Cuadra [38].

IV. Nutritional Adequacy

An often measured indicator of welfare is adequacy of food consumption. This is not surprising since food is perhaps the most fundamental of needs. Adequacy of food intake is usually assessed in terms of the calories, the proteins and the vitamins associated with food intake, which are then compared with certain established norms.

Nutritional standards are often also used to serve as a basis for poverty measures, which will be the approach adopted in the next section. Whether for evaluating food adequacy or for establishing poverty measures, the cogency of nutritional norms has been questioned [3], [4], [5], [40], [41]. The importance of taking great care in defining norms carefully and estimating consumption accurately has come to receive much attention.

In the case of Brazil several nutritional studies are available that use time series and cross sectional data. Many of these are cited in the recent World Bank study [20], which gives a comprehensive account of the nutritional situation in Brazil. This study makes extensive use of the ENDEF data on food consumption and the ENDEF's nutritional norms. In this section, we shall also present findings based on the ENDEF data and norms for all the ENDEF regions and areas and compare them with an alternative set of results.

A. Nutritional Norms

ENDEF provides data on ingestion requirements for the various regions and areas. These are minimum requirements for the people sampled in each location based on their age, sex, height, weight and activity level. The ENDEF requirements for calories and proteins are given in Annex Table 13.

The World Bank study [20] and Campino [4] point out that the requirements according to ENDEF are likely to be biased downwards. The degree of underestimation is more serious for the Northeast region. Several factors contribute to the overall underestimation of requirements. The use of height and weight alone does not allow for the additional nutritional needs of children and the malnourished. Correction of the activity level (or lack of it) also seems to understate the needs.

Comparing the ENDEF requirements with alternative standards, the possible underestimation in the former is brought out. The World Bank study [20] compares the ENDEF norms with consistently higher ones derived based on the FAO/WHO standards [7]. Campino [5] has developed an alternative set of norms based on a method for calculation of requirements established by the National Research Council (NRC) in the USA [29]. Campino's results are for the major ENDEF regions. In Annex Table 13 we present the requirements based on the NRC method for all the ENDEF sub-regions and areas as well. The requirements for the Northeast, according to these, are considerably higher than the ENDEF.

B. Achievement of Norms

ENDEF [12] provides data on calories and proteins consumed per person per day for all regions and areas. These estimates are based on estimated quantity of meals consumed at home and outside the home. Annex Table 13 shows how much these estimated consumption levels represent in percentage terms compared to alternative measures of requirements. Table IV.1 below summarizes these findings for the major regions and areas.

Based on the ENDEF requirements, calorie deficits are found only in Fortaleza, Salvador, Belem, and some other urban areas in Region VII. The nation as a whole shows a surplus of about 5%. The picture changes drastically, however, if the NRC-based requirements are used. Regions V, VII, VI and I (in that order) do not fulfill minimum requirements, with urban areas, in general, showing substantial deficits. The nation as a whole achieves only about 97% of the calorie requirements, with all the deficit (on the average) being distributed among the metropolitan and other urban areas.

No protein deficit is found in any location, whether based on the ENDEF or NRC requirements. The protein surplus derived on the ENDEF basis is cut down sharply, however, in using the alternative standard.

Sharp spatial differences emerge in the nutritional position in Brazil. As Table IV.1 shows, Regions II and III are best off nutritionally. These also happen to be the richer regions. It does not follow, however, that given the same real income, let alone money income, similar nutritional positions would be achieved elsewhere. The highly urbanized Regions I and VI, in spite of relatively high incomes, fail to meet calorie requirements. At the same time, it is true that the very poor regions also suffer the most serious problems of under-nourishment. Regions V and VII are the poorest and also worst off nutritionally. Region IV, also relatively poor, does better in its food consumption except in the case of its own metropolitan area.

Serious incidence of malnutrition is identified in the metropolitan areas in the poorest region V, Salvador, Recife, Fortaleza, and in Belem. The nutritional situation improves in the rural areas.

The World Bank study [20], presents findings on the calorie deficit at various ranges of the family expenditure distribution. At the 20th percentile, sizable per capita deficit is shown everywhere, in relation to FAO/WHO requirements. These deficits vary considerably but on average, the estimated per capita deficits in the metropolitan, other urban and rural areas of the country are, respectively, 492, 447 and 328. The most serious malnutrition among the poor is in the Northeast, particularly in Salvador and Fortaleza and Recife, with deficits, respectively, of 687, 668 and 598.

Table IV.1: PER CAPITA DAILY REQUIREMENTS[a] AND THEIR % ACHIEVED OF CALORIES AND PROTEINS: REGIONS AND AREAS OF BRAZIL (1974/75)

	Ingestion Requirement		Actual Ingestion		% of Requirement Ingested	
	Calories	Proteins	Calories	Proteins	Calories[b]	Proteins[b]
Regions						
Region I	2,244.4	44.4	2,066.3	65.2	92.0(102.9)	147.0(218.1)
Region II	2,026.5	44.4	2,123.7	64.1	105.2(102.6)	144.5(209.1)
Region III	2,257.9	44.1	2,360.8	70.1	104.5(107.0)	159.1(225.2)
Region IV	2,075.2	43.4	2,151.0	56.7	103.6(107.4)	130.7(189.0)
Region V	2,172.1	42.2	1,898.6	59.7	87.4(104.2)	141.5(209.2)
Region VI	2,212.3	42.9	1,944.4	62.3	87.8(101.8)	145.3(219.7)
Region VII	2,220.4	42.9	1,881.6	58.8	84.7(101.4)	136.9(216.8)
Areas						
Metropolitan	2,111.8	43.5	2,006.2	64.7	95.0(101.3)	148.8(218.0)
Other Urban	2,091.0	42.7	2,011.5	59.7	96.2(102.8)	139.8(204.7)
Rural	2,224.9	43.9	2,282.8	63.6	102.6(108.6)	144.8(210.3)
National	2,154.2	43.4	2,087.4	62.6	96.9(104.6)	144.3(210.6)

[a] Requirement according to Campino [5].
[b] Within brackets are the % achieved if ENDEF requirements were used instead of Campino.

Source: Annex Table 13.

V. Differences in Poverty Within Brazil

In this section we use the expenditure data and price indices discussed thus far to develop measures of poverty. The approach is to first construct expenditure levels that may be considered to represent absolute poverty levels [1]. These expenditure levels include minimum expenses on food and non-food categories. Given price differences, these "required" expenditures vary from place to place. Expenditure distribution data are then used to read off how many people actually spend less than the minimum requirements, giving the percentages of people considered poor across locations. An effort is also made to show by how much the expenditures of the poor fall short of the poverty thresholds.

Considering the subjectivity involved in defining absolute poverty, numerous poverty lines can be constructed even while confining oneself to an inexpensive consumption basket (Solorzano [38]). We have calculated various measures, but include three of them based on low cost food consumption baskets. The resulting poverty estimates should therefore be considered as conservative measures. The difference between the three measures arises from the choice of the minimum nutritional requirement, the food basket that achieves that requirement, and the differences in the price of the basket considered.

As mentioned in Section II, the price difference of one of the baskets (Type A below) is the basis for the food price index, considered

---

[1] See Ahluwalia [1], Anand [2], [16], Orshansky [30], Prado and Macedo [32], Sen [35], [36], Srinivasan [39], [40], Thomas [43].

relevant for the poor (Annex Table 5, column 2). This basket consists of food items in proportions actually consumed by people at the 20th percentile. A second basket (Type B below), aims at providing a lower cost figure by confining to items that contribute 75% of the calories. A third basket (Type C), is even more restrictive and low cost since only cereals -- in their actual proportion -- are considered.

Food price differences reflected by the cost of these baskets would be different from the food price index based on average consumption of all items at the mean (Section II), for three reasons. First, the baskets considered are different from those at the mean. Second, the prices of the items at the lower income groups are different than at the mean. (This may be due to quality differences and other factors.) Third, the average cost of a poverty diet at the national level is calculated using population weights rather than consumption weights for reasons given in Section II.

In all the three cases, the national non-food/food expenditure ratio of the 40th percentile times the non-food price index for the 20th percentile is used to derive minimum non-food allowances. The sum of the minimum food and non-food expenses gives the poverty lines.

A. Food Costs

The basis of our measure of the poverty line is the cost of buying a basic basket of food that provides the minimum requirement of calories and proteins. Two types of nutritional requirements are used. In one the results of the NRC-based Campino study [5] are used to allow for varying average nutritional needs in various locations. Alternatively, the same national requirement of FAO/WHO of 2,242 calories per person daily is used for all places. In all these cases, the protein requirements are automatically met, once the recommended calories are satisfied.

1. Type A Food Basket

The same FAO/WHO based national calorie requirement of 2,242 is considered for all places in constructing the type A basket. The food items used to meet this requirement are those consumed at the 20th percentile of the expenditure (monetary and non-monetary) distribution in each location. The quantity of these items is adjusted to meet the caloric requirements, which in most cases are achieved by people around the 40th percentile of the expenditure distribution. The prices used for costing this basket are those relevant to the 20th percentile. The cost of such a basket was calculated in the World Bank's Human Resources Special Report [20], which is given in Column 1 of Annex Table 17.

The poverty measure based on the type A food basket falls substantially below ones based on consumption patterns and prices at the mean (Solorzano [38]). At the same time, it is above the other measures reported in this study. Therefore it is considered the basis for a "medium level" poverty line.

An alternative measure was considered, based on the same food composition as in A, but allowing the nutritional requirements to vary according to [29]. The resulting differences are small, and so this measure is not used as a basis for the poverty line.

2. Type B Food Basket

In order to obtain a low cost diet, we choose for this basket only the major food items that actually provide 75% of calories per person at the mean in each location. The caloric requirements are allowed to vary according to the NRC-based calculation for each place. The quantity of items (that constitute 75% of calories) is adjusted proportionately so as to satisfy these calorie standards.

Annex Table 14 sets out the calorie composition of the type B basket by the major food items. Six to nine items provide 75% of calorie at the mean in each location. The importance of individual items varies considerably. Rice, bread and cassava are generally the most important items, in terms of calories, followed by sugar, beans and oils. Annex Table 15 provides details on the actual ordering of the various items across locations. Prices of these items are also given.

Type B basket for each place is costed out in Annex Table 16. The total cost per person is given in the final column and repeated in column 2 of Annex Table 18. Type B may be considered a low cost basket. It will be used as the basis for poverty line called "low 1."

3. Type C Food Basket

The lowest cost basket, type C, is composed only of cereals. The composition of cereals is determined by their actual proportion in the average diet in each location. The same 2,242 calories per day is sought to be met in all places by adjusting the quantities of cereals proportionately.

The cost of this basket was calculated in the World Bank study [20] and repeated in column 3 of Annex Table 17. This basket gives the lowest food cost, and hence is used as the basis for a "low 2" poverty line.

B. Non-Food Cost and Poverty Lines

Ideally a basic non-food basket should be defined and costed for each location as in the case of food. However, unlike the nutritional norms for food, no simple method exists to define a minimum non-food requirement. We have therefore used an observed non-food/food expenditure ratio for the poor to define a minimum required non-food allowance. We have then applied the non-food price indices developed in Section II to derive location specific non-food allowance.

In the final row under A' through C', national average requirements for non-food are given. Each of them is the product of the cost of a different food basket (type A through C) and the non-food/food expenditure ratio for the 20th percentile for the country as a whole of

0.7. The rest of the estimates under A' through C' are products of the national non-food requirement and the non-food price index at the 40th percentile. The variations in the non-food cost across locations reflect the spatial differences in non-food prices brought out in Section II.

The final columns in Annex Table 17 give the sum of the food costs for each basket type and its corresponding non-food cost. These are the poverty lines.

Table V.1 summarizes variations in the poverty lines for the major regions and areas. Regional differences are largest between the state of Sao Paulo and the Northeast. According to the three poverty lines, to buy the same quantities of minimum requirements, 50-60% higher nominal expenditures are needed in Sao Paulo state than in the Northeast. Urban-rural differences are greater. A similar basket of basic needs costs 70-90% more in the metropolitan areas than in the rural areas. The non-metropolitan urban areas fall roughly half way between these, and correspond to the national average.

C. Income Distribution

Apart from the cost of living-based poverty lines, data on regional income distribution are the chief information needed for constructing poverty measures. Income distribution schedules and measures for many of the ENDEF locations have been provided by Hoffman [17], Langoni [21] and Lodder [22] based on the 1970 Demographic Census. Discussion of Brazilian income distribution by locations and over time can also be found in Lluch [23], Macedo [25], Pfeffermann and Webb [31], Prado and Macedo [32].

To provide a consistent set of income distribution data for all the ENDEF locations which can then be compared with the ENDEF-based poverty lines, we tabulate family and per capita expenditure distributions directly from the ENDEF survey. These expenditure survey-based income distribution measures tend to show a lesser concentration of income compared to the demographic census-based estimates mentioned. One reason is that the expenditure data reflect permanent income better than the income data. Under the latter, income-in-kind and secondary incomes are often underreported. The expenditure-based distribution captures better the income of lower income groups thereby showing a lower concentration than the income-based distribution. The ENDEF also excludes those with insignificant expenditure, thereby understating the degree of concentration. Perhaps partly for these reasons, the ENDEF also shows a consistent and significant lower income concentration in the rural areas than in the urban zones, more than showed up in the income-based estimate mentioned above. Annex Table 18 sets out estimated Gini coefficients based on the ENDEF data and compares them with results obtained from the 1970 demographic census.

For the calculation of the Gini coefficients and for the estimation of poverty measures, we characterize the discrete expenditure distribution contained in the ENDEF in the form of a continuous Lorenz curve. We fitted a Lorenz curve with the nine observations for each location, using the method suggested in Ahluwalia [1] and Kakwani and Podder [19]. Discrepancies in the ENDEF data for extreme values (particularly the first two deciles and the last) affected the results in several cases. Geometric approximation of an expenditure distribution in the neighborhood of the poverty line had to be relied upon instead. This yielded an estimate of the percentage of people considered poor. In the neighborhood of this estimate a Lorenz curve was also geometrically fitted to enable the calculation of income of the poor.

D. Poverty Measures

A first measure of poverty is simply the percentage of people that falls below the poverty lines. Annex Table 17 and Table V.1 give three alternative poverty lines considered to be conservative estimates. From Annex Table 17, one may first choose "the medium" poverty line given by $A + A'$ for constructing a first poverty measure. Using the expenditure distribution, we read off the percentage and the number of people with expenditures below this threshold (see the previous sub-section) [1]/.

The results are given in Annex Table 19 and Table V.2. The "medium" definition implies that over 29% of the nation's population are poor comparable to the 28% estimated by Pfeffermann and Webb [31]. Their

---

1/ To see this, one may take the estimated poverty lines and compare with data on population by expenditure classes given in ENDEF (FIBGE[13]).

spatial distribution is very uneven, with great concentrations in the Northeast and rural areas. About 14 million people in the Northeast are considered poor, which is also about the size of rural population defined as poor.

Some degree of arbitariness involved in the choice and application of poverty lines is evident, in comparing results based on alternative thresholds. If the "low" definition of poverty given in section V.B were adopted, obviously much lower numbers would be defined as poor -- 23% - 24% according to Solorzano [38]. More liberal allowance for non-food expenditure would raise the poverty lines, and the number defined poor, probably significantly.

Given the tentative nature of the non-food price index in this paper, one should interpret carefully the poverty results based on them. Two results that have emerged on their basis are, however, important and robust. First, the relative positions of locations in the incidence of poverty are broadly maintained under alternative definitions of poverty. Thus, whether one adopts low, medium or high definitions of poverty, the types of disparities brought out in this paper are likely to remain.

Second, the use of the non-food price index, as presented in this paper, is likely to have given a more accurate presentation of the poverty profile than otherwise. Two alternatives would have been, first, to assume that all non-food expenditure differences are price differences, and second to assume that all non-food expenditure differences are real (quantity) differences. Under the first assumption, larger than necessary urban-rural differences in poverty lines would be adopted, resulting in smaller spatial differences in the incidence of poverty than found in this paper. Under the second assumption, a uniform non-food allowance would be built in with the poverty line resulting in wider spatial differences than suggested in this paper.

Both the above alternatives have been tried, in both cases assuming the same food expenditure. The summary results are given in Table V.2. The first column repeats results based on the "medium" poverty definition. The second column gives poverty estimates that would result if the actual non-food/food ratios in each location were assumed necessary to meet minimum needs. Thus the full difference in observed expenditures on non-food is assumed to be due to price differences, which in reality would be an exaggeration. Consequently poverty differences on this basis would understate true differences. This is readily seen by comparing the regions or urban-rural areas in Table V.2. The third column assumes the same non-food allowance calculated at the national level, as for the medium definition, to be sufficient in all regions. This presumes no spatial price differences, and as a result, exaggerates the variation in poverty. For instance, in the last column of Table V.2 the percentage defined poor in rural areas on the basis of this definition, is four times that in the metropolitan areas.

The above indices only dealt with the percentage of people considered poor. A second measure of poverty takes into account both the percentage of people who are poor and the extent of their poverty. The Sen Index given below (I) considers both these components of poverty.

$$I = \left(\frac{N_p}{N}\right) \left[\frac{Y^* - Y_p(1 - G_p)}{Y^*}\right] \qquad (V.1)$$

where N_p is the number of poor and N the total population; Y^* is the poverty line and Y_p the average income (expenditure) of the poor; G_p is the Gini coefficient of consumption of the poor.

If all poor have the same income ((i.e. $G_p = 0$)), the index is the product of the percentage of poor people and the proportion amount of income shortfall from the poverty line. If the distribution of income among the poor is also important, $(1 - G_p)$ weights Y_p such that a worse distribution results in a larger poverty index.

Suppose we ignore the distribution of income among the poor and express the poverty gap $(Y^* - Y_p)$ as a fraction of the average income of the location Y (rather than Y^*). This tells us the percentage of a location's existing total income that is needed to be directed to the poor to enable them to cross the poverty level. This index I′, taken from Thomas [43], is given below:

$$I' = \left(\frac{N_p}{N}\right) \left(\frac{Y^* - Y_p}{\bar{Y}}\right) \qquad (V.2)$$

where Y is the average income of the region.

Annex Table 19 and Table V.2 present estimates of equations (V.1) and (V.2) based on the "medium" poverty line. Broad differences in poverty implied by these indices are similar to the ones given by the percentage poor, but some of the urban-rural differences are reduced due to the better rural income distribution implied in the ENDEF. Some of the regional differences are augmented, also because some of the poorer regions have worse income distributions.

Referring to equation (V.2), it is indicated that in order to enable everyone to have income equal to or above a "medium" poverty line, over a 5% increase in annual national income is needed (over the actual increase in 1974/75), and all of this increase would go to the poor. The spatial distribution of this needed increase is very uneven, however. In the case of the Northeast the required increase is 10% compared to less than 2% in the state of Sao Paulo. For the rural areas as a whole a 10% increase is needed as compared to over 2% in the metropolitan areas.

TABLE V.1

FOOD COSTS AND POVERTY LINES

REGIONS	FOOD COST			TOTAL COST: POVERTY LINES		
	TYPE A	TYPE B	TYPE C	MEDIUM (TYPE A)	LOW 1 (TYPE B)	LOW 2 (TYPE C)
Region I	1,500	1,219	920	2,585	2,020	1,675
Region II	1,473	919	927	2,663	1,797	1,799
Region III	1,129	876	720	1,885	1,433	1,245
Region IV	932	748	701	1,631	1,264	1,187
Region V	969	668	723	1,620	1,148	1,176
Region VI	1,642	1,003	874	2,896	1,928	1,746
Region VII	846	1,146	904	1,730	1,798	1,519
Areas						
Metropolitan	1,537	1,149	966	2,831	2,104	1,866
Other Urban	1,094	813	844	1,941	1,438	1,313
Rural	919	643	641	1,562	1,117	1,088
National Average	1,149	847	798	1,953	1,440	1,357

Source: Annex Table 17.

TABLE V.2

ALTERNATIVELY DEFINED POVERTY LINES

REGIONS	Uniform Non-Food Needs with Allowances for Price Differences 1/ Poverty Line	% Below	Non-Uniform Non-Food Allowance 2/ Poverty Line	% Below	Uniform Non-Food Allowance With No Price Difference 3/ Poverty Line	% Below
Region I	2,585	16	2,727	18	2,304	12
Region II	2,663	21	2,888	24	2,277	14
Region III	1,885	19	1,851	18	1,933	20
Region IV	1,631	29	1,331	21	1,736	32
Region V	1,620	48	1,346	37	1,773	54
Region VI	2,896	16	3,351	23	2,446	11
Region VII	1,730	15	1,434	9	1,650	13
Areas						
Metropolitan	2,831	17	2,900	19	2,341	12
Other Urban	1,942	23	1,886	21	1,898	22
Rural	1,562	39	1,414	31	1,723	48
National Average	1,953	29	1,953	29	1,953	29

*Note: all poverty lines adopt the same Type A food cost from Table V.1

1/ A+A' in Annex Table 17 and type A in Table V.1; this poverty line adopts the same non-food/food ratio, for all locations, but allows for price differences in non-food items.

2/ This poverty line uses each location's non-food/food ratio to calculate non-food needs. No further price adjustments are made.

3/ A single non-food/food ratio is used to calculate the same non-food allowances for all locations.

Source: Calculations for all ENDEF Sub-regions and areas.

TABLE V.3

POVERTY MEASURES

	"MEDIUM" POVERTY LINE		
REGIONS	% BELOW	POVERTY INDEX a/	INCOME DEFICIENCY % b/
REGION I	16	9.90	2.44
REGION II	21	8.13	1.61
REGION III	19	7.74	1.88
REGION IV	29	17.84	4.75
REGION V	48	25.91	9.97
REGION VI	16	6.63	1.17
REGION VII	15	12.68	2.75
AREAS			
Metropolitan	17	10.41	2.18
Other Urban	23	13.64	4.52
Rural	39	18.65	10.06
NATIONAL AVERAGE	29	15.45	5.05

a/ Sen Index (I) in equation (V.1) multiplied by 100.

b/ Equation (V.2) X 100.

Source: Annex Table 19.

TABLE 1

ENDEF'S CLASSIFICATION OF REGIONS /a

BRAZIL (1974)

Regions	% of National Population	% of Region's Population
Region I - Rio de Janeiro	9.88	100.00
Metropolitan	(7.78)	78.76
Other Urban	(1.13)	11.53
Rural	(0.95)	9.71
Region II - São Paulo	20.45	100.00
Metropolitan	(9.06)	44.30
Other Urban	(7.70)	37.66
Rural	(3.69)	18.04
Region III - Paraná, Santa Catarina, R.Grande do Sul	18.88	100.00
Porto Alegre	(1.73)	9.29
Curitiba	(0.88)	4.74
Other Urban	(6.33)	33.90
Rural	(9.73)	52.07
Region IV - Espírito Santo, Minas Gerais	14.13	100.00
Belo Horizonte	(2.00)	14.16
Other Urban	(5.63)	39.89
Rural	(6.49)	45.95
Region V - Maranhão, Piauí, Ceará, R.G.do Norte, Paraíba, Pernambuco, Alagoas, Sergipe e Bahia	31.57	100.00
Salvador	(1.34)	4.27
Recife	(2.08)	6.61
Fortaleza	(1.16)	3.70
Other Urban	(9.12)	28.89
Rural	(17.85)	56.54
Region VI - Distrito Federal	0.73	100.00
Region VII /b - Rondonia, Acre, Roraima, Pará, Amapá, Goiás, Mato Grosso	4.33	100.00
Belém	(0.80)	18.72
Other Urban /c	(1.21)	27.93
Other Urban /d	(2.31)	53.35
National Population	100.00	

/a Calculated from ENDEF data on distribution of families and average family size by areas. the results may not correspond exactly with other sources. For consistency, regional populations were recalculated from their components.
/b Excludes rural areas in this and all remaining tables.
/c Rondônia, Acre, Amazonas, Roraima, Pará e Amapa.
/d Goiás, Mato Grosso.

Sources: Calculated from FIBGE [13].

TABLE 2

ENDEF'S CLASSIFICATION OF AREAS [a]

BRAZIL (1974)

	% of National Population	% of Areas Population
Metropolitan Areas	27.67	100.00
Rio de Janeiro	(7.80)	28.18
São Paulo	(9.80)	32.82
Porto Alegre	(1.74)	6.29
Curitiba	(0.89)	3.21
Belo Horizonte	(2.00)	7.24
Salvador	(1.35)	4.88
Recife	(2.09)	7.56
Fortaleza	(1.17)	4.22
Brasília	(0.74)	2.66
Belém	(0.81)	2.94
Other Urban Areas	33.52	100.00
Region I	(1.14)	3.41
Region II	(7.72)	23.02
Region III	(6.35)	18.93
Region IV	(5.65)	16.85
Region V	(9.14)	27.26
Region VII [b]	(1.21)	3.62
Region VII [c]	(2.32)	6.91
Rural Areas	(38.81)	100.00
Region I	(0.96)	2.48
Region II	(3.70)	9.53
Region III	(9.75)	25.13
Region IV	(6.51)	16.77
Region V	(17.89)	46.09
Total	100	

[a] Calculated from ENDEF data in distribution of families and average family size by areas; the results may not correspond exactly with other sources.
[b] Rondônia, Acre, Amazonas, Roraima, Pará, Amapá
[c] Goiás, Mato Grosso

Source: Calculated from FIBGE [13].

Table 3

Price Indices for Major Food Categories /a : Brazil (1974/75)
(National Average = 100)

	Cereals	Roots	Sugar	Beans	Vegetables	Fruits	Meat and Fish	Eggs and Milk	Oil and Fats	Drinks and Others	Total
Region I											
Metropolitan Rio	105.23	87.87	106.52	142.97	100.41	123.34	116.94	103.57	105.73	107.30	110.84
Other Urban	109.98	134.62	107.28	149.56	103.29	124.72	117.50	105.06	106.35	106.39	115.00
	102.23	115.74	99.95	151.58	91.60	124.84	108.60	99.70	105.20	99.68	107.92
Rural	90.18	111.72	102.08	108.37	85.46	126.29	96.46	102.21	103.20	107.73	99.38
Region II											
Metropolitan Sao Paulo	110.85	140.80	110.40	148.65	102.22	120.17	118.99	110.15	116.87	101.41	116.61
	121.79	153.57	122.14	149.39	105.86	127.63	124.92	128.23	119.15	100.27	124.12
Other Urban	105.32	148.87	120.48	154.21	99.19	116.64	116.37	112.48	115.21	103.03	115.77
Rural	106.42	128.79	103.31	136.45	98.50	124.50	106.81	97.80	117.63	102.10	109.33
Region III											
Curitiba	93.27	95.07	102.27	112.75	97.90	113.51	90.48	91.21	96.69	96.62	95.63
Porto Alegre	109.84	116.47	109.53	127.30	97.10	144.11	99.00	97.86	101.36	90.36	105.55
	94.68	113.23	124.54	134.88	111.59	110.01	110.99	108.68	106.43	97.73	108.30
Other Urban	92.46	99.16	106.80	120.81	98.45	106.26	92.35	103.65	99.00	91.61	97.65
Rural	96.87	93.80	99.05	106.75	93.85	117.83	82.44	82.52	97.40	99.44	92.77
Region IV											
Belo Horizonte	95.72	102.91	105.04	74.02	89.72	114.86	93.47	95.09	107.39	100.10	95.94
	101.65	122.62	104.11	116.47	103.47	147.61	121.28	103.77	105.74	97.14	111.68
Other Urban	100.00	111.15	101.16	91.89	93.97	103.27	105.65	103.38	119.74	99.70	102.73
Rural	98.31	91.91	113.75	64.78	86.68	105.90	93.63	85.82	108.31	102.70	94.09
Region V											
Fortaleza	88.23	114.69	113.76	86.73	115.64	98.12	93.89	107.09	137.82	98.94	100.03
Recife	93.16	131.41	116.48	93.08	123.29	126.68	103.65	121.24	113.55	97.04	106.36
Salvador	101.31	124.75	112.51	98.25	112.33	115.62	113.96	115.70	124.25	99.54	110.13
	116.15	140.77	112.20	141.30	122.07	120.17	121.82	120.14	129.86	116.30	120.47
Other Urban	94.06	112.29	114.50	88.50	106.56	88.77	98.34	100.35	124.75	99.37	100.53
Rural	87.96	127.31	114.50	84.76	134.82	101.03	61.01	102.35	144.25	102.22	92.41
Region VI	103.71	157.31	121.00	126.80	113.46	137.75	136.38	108.37	132.23	100.34	121.84
Region VII											
Belem	104.95	201.67	133.00	141.37	141.63	135.07	105.30	107.72	124.93	107.93	118.16 /b
	100.27	200.53	144.60	131.87	172.31	166.67	107.24	130.01	120.11	95.33	121.74 /b
Other Urban	104.47	239.57	170.19	160.91	198.00	150.33	112.14	106.10	134.00	110.39	129.50 /b
Other Urban	110.96	194.56	122.92	124.81	124.20	131.45	100.62	108.43	123.96	107.41	117.73 /b
National Average	100.00	100.00	100.00	100.00	100.00	100.00	100.00	100.00	100.00	100.00	100.00

/a See [13] for definitions. The ten major categories below are subgroups of about 120 food items.
/b Deleting roots, price indices of 114.01, 117.83, 124.04 and 113.92 are obtained respectively.

Sources: ENDEF.

Table 4

Median Rents for Comparable Housing in 126 Municipalities* - 1970

	Median Rent ($ Cr/month)	Price Index /b
Region I		
Metropolitan Rio	181.82	137
Other Urban /a	85.41	64
(Volta Redonda)	(91.36)	(69)
(Valenca)	(69.47)	(52)
Region II		
Metropolitan Sao Paulo	167.05	126
Other Urban /a	84.37	64
(Perreira Barreto)	(162.54)	(123)
(Campinas)	(124.35)	(94)
(Ribeiro Preto)	(105.86)	(80)
(Sorocaba)	(81.82)	(62)
(Sertaozinho)	(53.41)	(40)
Region III		
Porto Alegre	162.21	122
Curitiba	139.20	105
Other Urban /a	102.10	77
(Londrina)	(121.45)	(92)
(Rio Grande)	(101.13)	(76)
(Florianopolis)	(65.57)	(49)
Region IV		
Belo Horizonte	139.08	105
Other Urban /a	64.62	49
(Vitoria)	(98.03)	(74)
(Ouro Preto)	(56.47)	(43)
(Nanugra)	(29.13)	(22)
Region VI (Brasilia)	193.58	146
Region VII		
Goias	164.79	124
Anapolis	106.00	80
Average	132.52	100

* Excluding Region V.

/a Average for a number of "non-metropolitan" urban areas.
/b With average for the 126 municipalities = 100.

Source: Adapted from 1970 Demographic Census, provided by Vernon Henderson.

Table 5

Estimated Food, Non-Food and Overall Price Indices for Regions and Areas: Brazil (1974/75)
(Base: National Average = 100)

	I. Food A. Average National Basket /a	I. Food B. Location Specific Basket of 20th Perc. /b	II. Non-Food /d A. Mean	II. Non-Food /d B. 40th Perc.	III. Overall /e A. Average National Food + 40th Perc. Non-Food	III. Overall /e B. Low Cost 20th Perc. Food + 40th Perc. Non-Food
Region I	111	126	221	175	151	162
Metropolitan Rio	115	135	240	194	165	179
Other Urban	108	107	121	103	105	104
Rural	99	78	89	75	85	77
Region II	116	123	183	148	138	141
Metropolitan Sao Paulo	124	146	262	207	179	193
Other Urban	116	110	134	113	114	112
Rural	109	96	92	78	90	87
Region III	96	95*	117	94	95	94
Curitiba	106	107	210	133	125	126
Porto Alegre	108	138	220	158	144	153
Other Urban	98	103	127	107	105	106
Rural	93	81	84	71	80	76
Region IV	96	82	95	87	90	85
Belo Horizonte	112	110	172	133	127	127
Other Urban	103	83	89	99	100	94
Rural	94	73	77	65	78	70
Region V	100	83	n.a.	n.a.	n.a.	n.a.
Fortaleza	106	91	100	101	103	98
Recife	110	107	123	111	111	110
Salvador	120	137	164	133	130	134
Other Urban	100	83	91	100	100	93
Rural	92	75	n.a.	n.a.	n.a.	n.a.
Region VI	121	140	196	156	146	152
Region VII	118 (114)/c	78	115	110	113	100
Belem	122 (118)/c	85	120	138	132	120
Other Urban	130 (124)/c	74	111	121	124	102
Other Urban	118 (114)/c	78	116	110	113	99
Areas						
Metropolitan	n.a.	131	217	161	n.a.	154
Other Urban	n.a.	93	111	105	n.a.	100
Other Rural	n.a.	78	n.a.	n.a.	n.a.	n.a.

n.a. - not available. * - See Table II.1 for comments.

/a Based on prices of individual food items, obtained by dividing average food expenditures by average food quantities in the ENDEF data [12], [13]; see Annex Table 3.
/b Based on World Bank [20], page 67, Table 20, cost of type 2 diet. The index shows the price variance of a low income food basket (defined as the typical diet of the 20th percentile that just meets the FAO/WHO minimum calorie norm of 2,242, which happens in most cases around the 40th percentile.
/c Excluding roots; see Table 3.
/d See text for explanations. A below based on total non-food expenditure, and B on monetary expenditure alone.
/e Weighted averages of the food and non-food price indices.

Sources: FIBGE [12], Tables 8 through 12; [13], Table 4; and World Bank [20].

TABLE 6
ANNUAL PER CAPITA MONETARY EXPENDITURE BY REGIONS AND AREAS - BRAZIL (1974/75) /a
(CRUZEIROS, 1974)

	Food (1)	Non-Food Global/b (2)	Non-Food Current/c (3)	Non-Food Consumption/d (4)	Total Global (1)+(2)	Total Current (1)+(3)	Total Consumption (1)+(4)
Region I	1,877	6,572	4,447	3,736	8,449	6,324	5,613
Metropolitan Rio	1,955	7,356	4,949	4,180	9,311	6,904	6,135
Other Urban	1,292	3,534	2,408	2,095	4,826	3,700	3,387
Rural	792	1,275	853	772	2,067	1,645	1,564
Region II	1,435	5,699	3,324	2,834	7,134	4,760	4,269
Metropolitan S. Paulo	2,062	9,805	5,571	4,676	11,868	7,634	6,739
Other Urban	1,367	4,351	2,655	2,313	5,718	4,022	3,680
Rural	918	1,922	1,244	1,132	2,841	2,163	2,051
Region III	981	3,609	2,122	1,869	4,590	3,104	2,851
Curitiba	1,659	7,948	4,483	3,774	9,608	6,143	5,434
Porto Alegre	1,855	7,765	4,792	4,056	9,620	6,647	5,911
Other Urban	1,239	4,895	2,783	2,429	6,134	4,022	3,699
Rural	662	1,878	1,143	1,067	2,541	1,806	1,730
Region IV	860	2,909	1,798	1,591	3,770	2,658	2,452
Belo Horizonte	1,437	7,114	3,901	3,343	8,551	5,338	4,780
Other Urban	1,083	3,297	2,138	1,919	4,381	3,221	3,002
Rural	490	1,267	855	767	1,757	1,345	1,257
Region V	697	1,338	978	868	2,035	1,675	1,565
Fortaleza	1,062	2,601	1,813	1,582	3,663	2,876	2,645
Recife	1,300	3,471	2,515	2,162	4,772	3,816	3,463
Salvador	1,482	5,607	3,588	3,069	7,090	5,071	4,552
Other Urban	923	1,632	1,230	1,096	2,556	2,154	2,020
Rural	427	533	418	386	960	845	813
Region VI	1,518	5,975	4,177	3,569	7,494	5,696	5,088
Region VII	1,306	3,583	2,425	2,159	4,889	3,731	3,465
Belém	1,377	3,079	2,318	1,995	4,456	3,695	3,373
Other Urban /e	1,176	2,259	1,622	1,397	3,435	2,799	2,574
Other Urban /e	1,158	3,931	2,530	2,301	5,089	3,688	3,460
AREAS							
Metropolitan	1,798	7,446	4,572	3,865	9,245	6,371	5,664
Other Urban	1,150	3,403	2,149	1,896	4,554	3,300	3,046
Rural	552	1,145	763	702	1,698	1,316	1,255
National Average	1,073	3,528	2,218	1,920	4,602	3,292	2,994

/a See Annex Table 1 for definitions.

/b Global: Current (defined below) plus all other acquisitions.

/c Current: Consumption (below) plus taxes and contributions.

/d Consumption: Food, clothing, housing, health, personal care, transport, education and others.

/e See Annex Table 1 for definitions.

Source: Calculated from: ENDEF, FIBGE 1978, "Despesas das Familias", Table 3.

TABLE 7
ANNUAL PER CAPITA TOTAL EXPENDITURE (MONETARY AND NON MONETARY) BY REGIONS
BRAZIL (1974/75)
(CRUZEIROS 1974)

	Food (1)	Non Food Global[b] (2)	Non Food Current[c] (3)	Non Food Consumption[d] (4)	Total Global (1)+(2)	Total Current (1)+(3)	Total Consumption (1)+(4)
Region I	2,132	7,886	5,737	5,026	10,018	7,869	8,330
Metropolitan Rio	2,219	8,768	6,381	5,572	10,988	8,601	7,792
Other Urban	1,537	4,247	3,065	2,752	5,784	4,603	4,290
Rural	1,193	1,607	1,172	1,092	2,801	2,366	2,285
Region II	1,674	6,841	4,419	3,928	8,516	6,093	5,602
Metropolitan S.Paulo	2,228	11,718	7,399	6,505	13,946	9,627	8,733
Other Urban	1,603	5,275	3,538	3,197	6,879	5,142	4,801
Rural	1,491	2,329	1,646	1,534	3,820	3,137	3,025
Region III	1,542	4,265	2,746	2,493	5,807	4,288	4,035
Curitiba	1,900	9,343	5,785	5,076	11,244	7,685	6,977
Porto Alegre	2,093	9,236	6,207	5,471	11,329	8,300	7,565
Other Urban	1,542	5,668	3,532	3,179	7,210	5,074	4,721
Rural	1,515	2,290	1,525	1,449	3,805	3,040	2,964
Region IV	1,323	3,408	2,285	2,079	4,732	3,609	3,402
Belo Horizonte	1,611	8,374	5,143	4,585	9,985	6,755	6,196
Other Urban	1,363	3,855	2,675	2,456	5,218	4,039	3,820
Rural	1,200	1,491	1,067	979	2,692	2,268	2,175
Region V	1,029	1,616	1,234	1,123	2,645	2,357	2,152
Fortaleza	1,261	3,163	2,328	2,097	4,425	3,590	3,359
Recife	1,452	4,147	3,122	2,769	4,600	4,574	4,221
Salvador	1,599	7,166	4,857	4,338	8,765	6,456	5,937
Other Urban	1,147	1,913	1,501	1,368	3,061	2,649	2,515
Rural	860	648	531	499	1,508	1,391	1,359
Region VI	1,711	7,599	5,707	5,100	9,310	7,419	6,811
Region VII	1,681	4,340	3,163	2,897	6,021	4,844	4,578
Belém	1,527	3,827	3,057	2,735	5,355	4,585	4,262
Other Urban[e]	1,466	2,784	2,139	1,914	4,250	3,605	3,380
Other Urban[e]	1,602	4,703	3,275	3,047	6,305	4,878	4,649
Areas							
Metropolitan	1,970	8,917	5,989	5,271	10,915	7,987	7,268
Other Urban	1,420	4,030	2,752	2,498	5,450	4,172	3,918
Rural	1,150	1,386	1,047	932	2,537	2,197	2,082
National Average	1,441	4,218	2,880	2,581	5,660	4,321	4,023

a/ See Annex Table 1 for definitions.
b/ Global: Current (see below) plus all other acquisitions.
c/ Current: Consumption (see below) plus taxes and contributions.
d/ Consumption: Food, clothing, housing, health, personal care, transport, education and others.
e/ See Annex Table 1 for definitions.

Source: Calculated from ENDEF, FIBGE/1978, "Despesas das Famílias", Table 4.

TABLE 8

SPATIAL DIFFERENCES OF THE ANNUAL PER CAPITA AVERAGE EXPENDITURE:
BRAZIL (1974/75)
BASE: NATIONAL AVERAGE = 100

	Global[a]		Current[a]		Consumption[a]	
	(1)	(2)	(1)	(2)	(1)	(2)
Region I	177	183	182	192	207	187
Metropolitan Rio Janeiro	194	202	199	209	193	204
Other Urban	102	104	106	112	106	113
Rural	49	44	54	49	56	52
Region II	150	155	140	144	139	142
Metropolitan São Paulo	246	257	222	231	217	225
Other Urban	121	124	118	122	119	122
Rural	67	61	72	65	75	68
Region III	102	99	99	94	100	95
Curitiba	198	208	177	186	173	181
Porto Alegre	200	209	192	201	188	197
Other Urban	127	133	117	122	117	122
Rural	67	55	70	54	73	57
Region IV	83	81	83	80	84	81
Belo Horizonte	176	185	156	162	154	159
Other Urban	92	95	93	97	94	100
Rural	47	38	52	40	54	41
Region V	46	44	54	50	53	52
Fortaleza	78	79	83	87	83	88
Recife	81	103	105	115	104	115
Salvador	154	154	149	154	147	152
Other Urban	54	55	61	65	62	67
Rural	26	20	32	25	33	27
Region VI	164	162	171	173	169	169
Region VII	106	106	112	113	113	115
Belém	94	96	106	112	105	112
Other Urban	75	74	83	85	84	85
Other Urban Areas	111	110	112	112	115	115
Metropolitan	192	200	184	193	180	189
Other Urban	96	98	96	100	97	101
Rural	44	36	50	39	51	41

[a] See Annex Table 6 for definitions.

Note: (1) indicates monetary and non-monetary; (2) is only monetary.

Source: Based on Annex Tables 6 and 7.

TABLE 9

ANNUAL PER CAPITA MEAN MONETARY CURRENT EXPENDITURE: BRAZIL (1974/75)

	Current Expenditure			% Spent	
	Non Food	Food	Total	Non Food	Food
Region I	4,447	1,877	6,324	70.31	29.69
Metropolitan Rio Janeiro	4.949	1,955	6,904	71.68	28.32
Other Urban	2,408	1,292	3,706	65.08	34.92
Rural	853	792	1,645	51.85	48.15
Region II	3,324	1,435	4,760	69.83	30.17
Metropolitan São Paulo	5,571	2.062	7,634	72.98	27.02
Other Urban	2,655	1,367	4,022	66.01	33.99
Rural	1,244	918	2,163	57.51	42.49
Region III	2,122	981	3,104.	68.36	31.64
Curitiba	4,483	1,659	6,143	72.98	27.02
Porto Alegre	4,792	1,855	6,647	72.09	27.91
Other Urban	2,783	1,239	4.022	69.19	30.81
Rural	1,143	662	1,806	63.29	36.71
Region IV	1,798	860	2,658	67.64	32.36
Belo Horizonte	3,901	1,437	5,338	73.08	26.92
Other Urban	2,138	1,083	3.221	66.38	33.62
Rural	855	490	1,345	63.36	36.64
Region V	978	697	1,675	58.39	41.61
Fortaleza	1,813	1,062	2,876	63.04	36.96
Recife	2,515	1,300	3,816	65.91	34.09
Salvador	3,588	1,482	5,071	70.76	29.24
Other Urban	1,230	923	2,154	57.10	42.90
Rural	418	427	845	49.47	50.53
Region VI	4,177	1,518	5,696	73.33	26.67
Region VII	2,425	1,306	3,731	65.00	35.00
Belem	2,318	1,377	3,695	62.73	37.27
Other Urban	1,622	1,176	2,798	57.79	42.21
Other Urban	2,530	1,158	3.688	68.60	31.40
Areas					
Metropolitan	4,572	1,798	6,371	71.76	28.24
Other Urban	2,149	1,150	3,300	65.12	34.88
Rural	763	552	1,316	57.98	42.02
National Average	2,218	1,073	3,292	67.38	32.62

Source: Calculated from ENDEF.

TABLE 10

ANNUAL PER CAPITA MEAN CURRENT EXPENDITURE (MON. PLUS NON-MON): BRAZIL (1974/75)

	Current Expenditure			% Spent	
	Non Food	Food	Total	Non Food	Food
Region I	5,737	2,132	7,869	72.91	27.09
Metropolitan Rio Janeiro	6,381	2,219	8,601	74.19	25.81
Other Urban	3,065	1,537	4,603	66.59	33.41
Rural	1,172	1,193	2,366	49.54	50.46
Region II	4,419	1,674	6,093	72.53	27.47
Metropolitan São Paulo	7,399	2,228	9,627	76.86	23.14
Other Urban	3,538	1,603	5,142	68.81	31.19
Rural	1,646	1,491	3,137	52.47	47.53
Region III	2,746	1,542	4.288	64.04	35.96
Curitiba	5,785	1,900	7,685	75.28	24.72
Porto Alegre	6,207	2,093	8,300	74.78	25.22
Other Urban	3,532	1,542	5,074	69.61	30.39
Rural	1,525	1,515	3.040	50.16	49.84
Region IV	2,285	1,323	3,609	63.31	36.69
Belo Horizonte	5,143	1,611	6,755	76.14	23.86
Other Urban	2,675	1,363	4,039	66.23	33.77
Rural	1,067	1,200	2,268	47.05	52.95
Region V	1,234	1,029	2,357	52.35	47.65
Fortaleza	2,328	1,261	3,590	64.85	35.15
Recife	3,122	1,452	4,574	68.26	31.74
Salvador	4,857	1,599	6,456	75.23	24.77
Other Urban	1,501	1,147	2,649	56.66	43.34
Rural	531	860	1,391	38.17	61.83
Region VI	5,707	1,711	7,419	76.92	23.08
Region VII	3,163	1,681	4,844	65.30	34.70
Belém	3,057	1,527	4,585	66.67	33,33
Other Urban	2,139	1,466	3,605	59.33	40.67
Other Urban	3,275	1,602	4,878	67.14	32.86
Areas					
Metropolitan	5,989	1,998	7,987	74.98	25.02
Other Urban	2,752	1,420	4,172	65.96	34.04
Rural	1,047	1,150	2,197	47.66	52.34
National Average	2,880	1,441	4,321	66.65	33.35

Source: Calculated from ENDEF.

TABLE 11

PERCENTAGE DISTRIBUTION IN CURRENT EXPENDITURE OF MAJOR ITEMS
BRAZIL (1974/75)

REGIONS	FOOD	HOUSING	CLOTHING	TRANSPORT	HEALTH	EDUCATION	RECREATION
REGION I	27.09	33.49	6.96	6.71	6.35	2.72	1.86
Metropolitan Rio	25.81	34.26	6.85	6.90	6.35	2.72	1.92
Other Urban	33.41	28.63	8.53	5.27	6.67	3.18	1.58
Rural	50.45	22.07	6.70	4.59	5.70	1.50	0.94
REGION II	27.48	34.09	7.33	7.21	6.12	2.35	1.53
Metropolitan S.Paulo	23.48	36.26	7.06	8.16	5.88	2.48	1.66
Other Urban	31.18	32.74	7.67	5.89	6.64	2.43	1.47
Rural	47.52	22.37	8.21	4.59	6.12	1.15	0.75
REGION III	35.96	26.87	8.60	6.01	6.77	1.87	1.40
Curitiba	24.76	33.78	8.14	6.88	5.74	2.56	1.69
Porto Alegre	25.22	32.61	7.79	8.13	5.55	2.70	2.09
Other Urban	30.39	29.27	9.37	6.03	6.83	2.16	1.64
Rural	49.84	19.87	8.26	4.75	7.54	0.97	0.74
REGION IV	36.67	25.76	8.92	5.34	6.99	2.36	1.52
Belo Horizonte	23.85	34.06	8.56	6.25	6.29	3.17	2.30
Other Urban	33.76	27.55	9.42	5.21	7.37	2.78	1.67
Rural	52.95	15.41	8.49	4.70	7.05	0.97	0.58
REGION V	45.47	23.31	8.58	4.29	5.64	1.88	1.29
Fortaleza	35.14	28.85	7.56	5.98	5.74	2.92	2.44
Recife	31.76	29.30	7.59	7.27	6.14	3.18	1.89
Salvador	24.77	37.40	7.82	6.90	5.56	3.28	1.78
Other Urban	43.32	23.63	9.56	4.07	6.18	2.07	1.37
Rural	61.84	14.81	8.45	2.16	4.92	0.53	0.60
REGION VI	23.07	38.58	6.27	7.34	5.66	2.57	2.11
REGION VII	34.07	29.19	9.06	5.07	6.93	2.04	1.87
Belém	33.32	32.09	6.78	5.81	5.86	2.27	2.36
Other Urban	40.67	27.64	7.78	3.53	6.00	1.34	1.57
Other Urban	32.85	28.84	10.30	5.42	7.64	2.23	1.83

Source: FIBGE [13], Table 8.

Table 12

Estimated Annual Per Capita Current Expenditure [a] at the Mean
Brazil (1974/75)
(Cruzeiros 1974)

	Food Nominal	Food Real [b]	Non-Food Nominal	Non-Food Real [b]	Total Nominal	Total Real
Region I [c]	1,895	1,707	5,100	2,914	6,995	4,621
	(2,132)	(1,921)	(5,737)	(3,278)	(7,869)	(5,199)
Metropolitan Rio	2,219	1,930	6,381	3,289	8,601	5,219
Other Urban	1,537	1,423	3,065	2,973	4,603	4,396
Rural	1,193	1,205	1,172	1,563	2,366	2,768
Region II	1,674	1,443	4,419	2,985	6,093	4,428
Metropolitan Sao Paulo	2,228	1,797	7,399	3,574	9,627	5,371
Other Urban	1,603	1,382	3,538	3,131	5,142	4,513
Rural	1,491	1,368	1,646	2,110	3,137	3,478
Region III	1,542	1,606	2,746	2,921	4,288	4,527
Curitiba	1,900	1,792	5,785	4,350	7,685	6,142
Porto Alegre	2,093	1,937	6,207	3,928	8,300	5,765
Other Urban	1,542	1,573	3,532	3,301	5,074	4,874
Rural	1,515	1,629	1,525	2,148	3,040	3,777
Region IV	1,323	1,378	2,285	2,626	3,609	4,004
Belo Horizonte	1,611	1,438	5,143	3,867	6,755	5,305
Other Urban	1,363	1,323	2,675	2,702	4,039	4,025
Rural	1,200	1,277	1,067	1,642	2,268	2,919
Region V	1,029	1,029	1,234	n.a.	2,357	n.a.
Fortaleza	1,261	1,190	2,328	2,305	3,590	3,495
Recife	1,452	1,320	3,122	2,812	4,574	4,132
Salvador	1,599	1,333	4,857	3,652	6,456	4,985
Other Urban	1,147	1,147	1,501	1,501	2,649	2,648
Rural	860	935	531	n.a.	1,391	n.a.
Region VI	1,711	1,414	5,707	3,658	7,418	5,072
Region VII	1,681	1,425	3,163	2,875	4,844	4,300
Belem	1,527	1,251	3,057	2,215	4,585	3,466
Other Urban	1,466	1,128	2,139	1,768	3,605	2,896
Other Urban	1,602	1,358	3,275	2,977	4,878	4,335
Areas						
Metropolitan	1,997	n.a.	5,989	3,720	7,986	n.a.
Other Urban	1,420	n.a.	2,752	2,620	4,172	n.a.
Other Rural	1,150	n.a.	1,047	n.a.	2,197	n.a.
National Average	1,441	1,441	2,880	2,880	4,321	4,321

n.a. - not available

[a] Monetary plus non-monetary.
[b] Nominal divided by the price indices in Table 4.
[c] There is some ambiguity about the appropriate family size for this region, given the two alternative per capita estimates.

Source: Calculated from FIBGE [13] and Annex Table 3

TABLE 13

ALTERNATIVES ESTIMATES OF DAILY MINIMUM REQUIREMENTS AND THEIR % ACHIEVED CALORIES AND PROTEIN FOR REGIONS AND AREAS: BRAZIL (1974)

	Requirements[a] Calories[b] (1) (2)	Proteins[c] (1) (2)	% Achieved (Ingested) Calories[b] (1) (2)	Proteins[c] (1) (2)
Region I	2,007.6 2,244.4	29.9 44.4	102.9 92.0	218.1 147.0
Metropolitan Rio	2,007.5 2,244.4	29.9 44.4	102.5 91.7	225.5 152.1
Other Urban	1,995.5 2,230.8	30.0 44.5	103.2 92.3	196.0 132.2
Rural	2,021.4 2,259.8	29.8 44.3	105.5 94.4	186.5 125.7
Region II	2,070.9 2,026.5	30.7 44.4	102.6 105.2	209.1 144.5
Metropolitan São Paulo	2,029.9 1,986.4	30.6 44.3	100.4 102.6	215.4 148.9
Other Urban	2,053.4 1,969.5	30.6 44.3	102.9 107.3	203.2 140.4
Rural	2,198.4 2,151.2	30.8 44.6	106.6 108.9	205.1 141.7
Region III	2,206.3 2,257.9	31.1 44.1	107.0 104.5	225.2 159.1
Curitiba	2,059.8 2,108.1	31.3 44.3	102.5 100.2	206.0 145.5
Porto Alegre	2,150.7 2,201.1	31.2 44.2	104.1 101.7	229.9 162.4
Other Urban	2,110.9 2,160.3	31.0 43.8	104.5 102.1	214.8 151.7
Rural	2,280.4 2,333.8	31.2 44.2	109.1 122.0	231.9 163.8
Region IV	2,003.6 2,075.2	30.0 43.4	107.4 103.6	189.0 130.7
Belo Horizonte	1,928.7 1,997.6	29.0 41.9	102.8 99.2	191.3 132.4
Other Urban	1,953.1 2,022.9	29.3 42.3	104.5 100.9	185.2 128.1
Rural	2,063.2 2,136.9	30.8 44.5	110.6 106.7	191.2 132.3
Region V	1,822.9 2,172.1	28.6 42.2	104.2 87.4	209.2 141.5
Fortaleza	1,704.8 2,031.4	27.2 40.2	98.7 82.8	207.4 140.3
Recife	1,823.2 2,172.5	27.8 41.1	101.7 85.8	217.1 146.8
Salvador	1,797.4 2,141.7	27.3 40.7	96.3 80.7	223.8 151.3
Other Urban	1,776.2 2,116.5	27.3 40.4	100.9 84.6	208.7 141.2
Rural	1,855.4 2,210.8	29.4 43.4	106.8 89.6	207.8 140.6
Region VI	1,910.4 2,212.3	28.3 42.9	101.8 87.8	219.7 145.3
Region VII	1,855.2 2,220.4	27.7 42.9	101.4 84.7	216.8 136.9
Belem	1,802.9 2,157.8	26.7 42.2	99.5 83.1	235.6 148.8
Other Urban	1,730.0 2,070.5	25.4 40.2	97.7 81.6	237.2 149.8
Other Urban Areas	1,934.2 2,314.9	28.1 44.5	103.7 86.6	201.7 127.4
Metropolitan	1,974.1 2,111.8	29.7 43.5	101.3 95.0	218.0 148.8
Other Urban	1,950.0 2,091.0	29.2 42.7	102.8 96.2	204.7 139.3
Rural	2,033.9 2,224.9	30.2 43.9	108.6 102.6	210.3 144.8
National Average	1,991.4 2,154.2	29.8 43.4	104.6 96.9	210.6 144.3

[a] (1): Requirements according to ENDEF and (2) according to National Research Council [26].
[b] Kilo calories
[c] Grams.

Source: A.C.C. Campino [5]; based on Tables 1, 2, 3 and 4.

TABLE 14

CALORIC COMPOSITION OF TYPE B [a] MINIMUM BASKET FOR REGIONS AND AREAS - BRAZIL (1974)

(K/CAL)

MAJOR FOOD ITEMS [b]

Regions	1	2	3	4	5	6	7	8	9	Total [c]
Region I	597.0	426.9	289.1	257.7	237.7	143.6	110.4	100.3	81.70	2,244.4
Metropolitan Rio	584.6	395.2	312.0	260.1	247.6	158.7	117.6	96.3	72.3	2,244.4
Other Urban	640.7	526.3	275.5	261.0	190.7	128.0	106.6	102.0	—	2,230.8
Rural	606.6	530.2	315.5	250.6	248.9	190.5	117.5	—	—	2,259.8
Region II	671.4	357.7	277.4	226.6	202.2	104.6	96.5	90.0	—	2,026.5
Metropolitan São Paulo	566.5	339.5	316.4	250.3	211.1	113.0	107.3	81.7	—	1,986.4
Other Urban	687.7	381.7	275.3	212.7	210.1	101.2	100.8	—	—	1,969.5
Rural	922.4	434.1	299.7	234.9	162.4	97.7	—	—	—	2,151.2
Region III	542.2	366.9	308.0	259.2	217.2	156.7	151.1	134.4	122.2	2,257.9
Porto Alegre	509.9	359.7	342.9	258.6	191.7	172.1	155.4	128.5	82.3	2,201.0
Curitiba	493.2	366.6	269.6	256.3	200.9	197.9	134.9	97.6	91.1	2,108.0
Other Urban	524.5	392.3	247.6	225.3	202.2	193.1	137.0	133.3	105.0	2,160.3
Rural	555.9	385.1	354.5	312.5	291.3	227.5	125.3	81.7	—	2,333.8
Region IV	610.1	374.9	300.6	236.7	203.9	126.8	116.3	105.9	—	2,075.2
Belo Horizonte	555.6	451.3	262.5	191.6	180.0	150.6	111.3	94.7	—	1,997.6
Other Urban	612.9	426.0	244.2	196.2	190.6	160.8	104.8	87.4	—	2,022.9
Rural	595.0	452.2	353.7	298.5	272.5	165.0	—	—	—	2,136.9
Region V	667.7	412.7	355.8	265.2	202.7	150.0	109.0	—	—	2,172.1
Salvador	530.8	438.6	328.8	248.7	243.9	202.0	148.9	—	—	2,141.7
Recife	599.5	441.2	318.7	233.8	197.7	176.4	107.3	98.0	—	2,172.5
Fortaleza	489.2	366.7	347.8	323.0	274.9	128.2	101.0	—	—	2,031.4
Other Urban	520.2	376.1	333.6	320.4	316.4	155.4	94.4	—	—	2,116.5
Rural	824.6	498.6	372.5	221.0	215.8	78.3	—	—	—	2,210.8
Region VI	699.7	351.7	298.9	296.5	271.0	151.1	143.4	—	—	2,212.3
Region VII	679.5	365.9	304.9	288.7	210.9	104.3	176.3	—	—	2,220.4
Belém	718.2	446.9	280.0	277.5	276.6	158.6	—	—	—	2,157.8
Other Urban	753.8	362.3	285.7	250.5	159.4	144.9	113.9	—	—	2,070.5
Other Urban	943.8	322.9	247.9	234.9	227.1	193.5	144.9	—	—	2,314.9

a/ Type B: Composed of major items that actually provide 75% of calories per person in each region and area.
b/ Food items in Annex Table 15 in the same order of importance according to calories provided detailed in that table.
c/ Equal to minimum daily calorie requirement per person.

Source: Based on ENDEF, FIBGE 1978, "Consumo Alimentar Antropometria", based on Table I.A; quantities of food that provide daily calorie requirements estimated in Table 12.

TABLE 15

PRICE PER 100 CALORIES OF ITEMS IN TYPE B[a] MINIMUM BASKET FOR REGIONS AND AREAS - BRAZIL (1974)

(CRUZEIROS 1974)

	1		2		3		4		5		6		7		8		9	
Region I	Rice	0.1020	Sugar	0.0518	Bread	0.1487	Beans	0.1375	Oils	0.1027	Beef	0.8463	Milk	0.2390	Wheat B	0.1370	Pork Fat	0.1189
Metropolitan Rio	Rice	0.1020	Sugar	0.0512	Bread	0.1396	Oils	0.0992	Beans	0.1359	Beef	0.8199	Milk	0.2291	Wheat B	0.1341	Margarine	0.1369
Other Urban	Rice	0.0941	Sugar	0.0381	Bread	0.1546	Beans	0.1205	Oils	0.0940	Pork Fat	0.1065	Wheat B	0.1387	Corn	0.0907	-	-
Rural	Rice	0.0770	Sugar	0.0397	Beans	0.1190	Cassava	0.0476	Corn	0.0816	Pork Fat	0.1441	Wheat B	0.1078	-	-	-	-
Region II	Rice	0.0791	Sugar	0.0337	Oils	0.0784	Bread	0.1230	Bread	0.1415	Milk	0.1664	Pork Fat	0.1123	Beef	0.6743	-	-
Metropolitan São Paulo	Rice	0.1001	Oils	0.0841	Sugar	0.0379	Bread	0.1784	Milk	0.1447	Milk	0.3050	Beef	0.0877	Wheat B	0.2125	-	-
Other Urban	Rice	0.0758	Sugar	0.0356	Oils	0.0816	Bread	0.1288	Beans	0.1456	Milk	0.2230	Pork Fat	0.1183	-	-	-	-
Rural	Rice	0.0896	Sugar	0.0399	Beans	0.1424	Pork Fat	0.1528	Oils	0.0967	Milk	0.1990	-	-	-	-	-	-
Region III	Rice	0.0825	Sugar	0.0452	Wheat A[d]	0.0608	Beans	0.1072	Pork Fat	0.1153	Corn	0.0710	Wheat B	0.1604	Oils	0.0907	Milk	0.1633
Curitiba	Rice	0.1055	Sugar	0.0402	Oils	0.0839	Bread	0.1606	Beans	0.1250	Wheat A	0.0540	Beef	0.0695	Wheat B	0.1658	Milk	0.2332
Porto Alegre	Rice	0.0826	Bread	0.1159	Sugar	0.0463	Oils	0.0886	Beef	0.6342	Milk	0.2202	Beans	0.1358	Wheat A	0.0564	Pork Fat	0.1109
Other Urban	Rice	0.0758	Sugar	0.0420	Bread	0.1222	Wheat A	0.0528	Oils	0.0823	Beans	0.1084	Pork Fat	0.3710	Pork Fat	0.0966	Milk	0.2800
Rural	Rice	0.0905	Wheat	0.0803	Oils	0.0504	Beans	0.1126	Corn	0.1114	Milk	0.1437	Cassava	0.1588	Cassava	0.0578	-	-
Region IV	Rice	0.0911	Sugar	0.0432	Beans	0.0915	Corn	0.1290	Corn	0.0891	Cassava	0.1533	Oils	0.0372	Oils	0.0976	-	-
Belo Horizonte	Rice	0.0921	Sugar	0.0342	Bread	0.1295	Beans	0.1111	Oils	0.1073	Milk	0.0852	Milk	0.2188	Wheat B	0.1071	-	-
Other Urban	Rice	0.0880	Sugar	0.0387	Beans	0.0988	Bread	0.1482	Oils	0.1230	Corn	0.0951	Corn	0.0991	Wheat B	0.1134	-	-
Rural	Rice	0.0942	Sugar	0.0547	Beans	0.0870	Corn	0.0902	Pork Fat	0.1635	Cassava	0.3024	-	-	-	-	-	-
Region V	Casava	0.0356	Beans	0.0748	Rice	0.0802	Sugar	0.0529	Bread	0.1315	Beef	0.0525	Beef	0.6345	-	-	-	-
Fortaleza	Rice	0.0919	Bread	0.0554	Beans	0.1056	Sugar	0.1171	Cassava	0.0968	Oils	0.7638	Beef	0.3009	-	-	-	-
Recife	Bread	0.1077	Sugar	0.0421	Cassava	0.0429	Beans	0.0983	Rice	0.1102	Oils	0.7371	Beef	0.1015	Wheat B	0.1136	-	-
Salvador	Bread	0.1270	Cassava	0.0332	Sugar	0.0443	Beef	0.6365	Beans	0.1111	Rice	0.1111	Oils	0.1023	-	-	-	-
Other Urban	Casava	0.0345	Sugar	0.0858	Bread	0.1421	Beans	0.0503	Beans	0.0911	Oils	0.6165	Oils	0.1106	-	-	-	-
Rural	Casava	0.0375	Beans	0.0775	Rice	0.0573	Sugar	0.0573	Corn	0.0500	Oils	0.1558	-	-	-	-	-	-
Region VI	Rice	0.0870	Sugar	0.0416	Oils	0.0872	Bread	0.1176	Beans	0.1065	Beef	0.6302	Milk	0.2120	-	-	-	-
Region VII	Rice	0.0953	Cassava	0.0893	Sugar	0.0589	Bread	0.1477	Oils	0.1460	Oils	0.1188	Beef	0.6635	-	-	-	-
Belem	Casava	0.0771	Bread	0.0902	Rice	0.0896	Beef	0.5837	Sugar	0.0540	Beans	0.1613	-	-	-	-	-	-
Other Urban	Casava	0.0822	Sugar	0.2483	Rice	0.1013	Sugar	0.0684	Beans	0.6692	Beef	0.1874	Fish	0.2302	-	-	-	-
Other Urban	Rice	0.0875	Sugar	0.0495	Beans	0.1169	Oils	0.1100	Pork Fat	0.1183	Bread	0.1783	Beef	0.5994	-	-	-	-

a/ Type B: Composed of major items that actually provide 75% of calories per person in each region and area.
b/ The numbers indicate the order of importance in terms of calories provided of food items.
c/ Wheat A - wheat flour.
d/ Wheat B - Macaroni from wheat.

Source: Based on ENDEF, FIBGE 1978; Based on "Consumo Alimentar Antropometria", Tables 1-A and 4; "Despesas da Família"; Table 5; Composição de Alimentos", Table 1.

TABLE 16

PER CAPITA COST OF TYPE B BASKET[a] FOR REGIONS AND AREAS - BRAZIL (1974)

(CRUZEIROS 1974)

MAJOR FOOD ITEMS[b]

Regions	1	2	3	4	5	6	7	8	9	Daily Total	Annual Total
Region I	0.61	0.22	0.43	0.35	0.24	1.22	0.26	0.14	0.10	3.34	1,219.1
Metropolitan Rio	0.62	0.20	0.44	0.26	0.34	1.30	0.27	0.13	0.10	3.64	1,328.6
Other Urban	0.62	0.20	0.43	0.31	0.18	0.14	0.15	0.09	-	2.10	766.5
Rural	0.47	0.21	0.38	0.12	0.20	0.27	0.13	-	-	1.78	649.7
Region II	0.53	0.12	0.22	0.28	0.29	0.17	0.11	-	-	2.52	919.8
Metropolitan São Paulo	0.57	0.29	0.12	0.45	0.31	0.34	0.89	0.61	-	3.14	1,146.1
Other Urban	0.52	0.14	0.22	0.27	0.31	0.23	0.12	0.17	-	1.82	664.3
Rural	0.83	0.17	0.43	0.31	0.16	0.19	-	-	-	2.09	762.9
Region III	0.45	0.17	0.19	0.28	0.25	0.11	0.24	0.12	0.22	2.40	876.0
Porto Alegre	0.42	0.42	0.16	0.23	1.22	0.38	0.21	0.07	0.09	3.20	1,168.0
Curitiba	0.52	0.15	0.23	0.41	0.25	0.11	0.93	0.16	0.21	2.97	1,084.1
Other Urban	0.40	0.16	0.30	0.12	0.17	0.21	0.51	0.13	0.29	2.29	835.9
Rural	0.50	0.31	0.18	0.35	0.32	0.33	0.20	0.05	-	2.24	817.6
Region IV	0.56	0.16	0.28	0.31	0.18	0.19	0.04	0.10	-	2.05	748.3
Belo Horizonte	0.51	0.15	0.34	0.21	0.19	0.13	0.24	0.10	-	1.87	682.6
Other Urban	0.54	0.16	0.24	0.29	0.23	0.15	0.10	0.10	-	1.81	660.7
Rural	0.56	0.25	0.31	0.27	0.44	0.49	-	-	-	2.32	846.8
Region V	0.24	0.31	0.29	0.14	0.27	0.08	0.69	-	-	1.83	668.0
Salvador	0.67	0.15	0.14	1.58	0.27	0.22	0.15	-	-	3.18	1,160.7
Recife	0.64	0.18	0.13	0.22	0.19	1.30	0.10	0.11	-	2.87	1,047.6
Fortaleza	0.44	0.20	0.36	0.37	0.26	0.97	0.30	-	-	2.90	1,058.5
Other Urban	0.17	0.32	0.47	0.16	0.28	0.95	0.10	-	-	2.45	894.3
Rural	0.30	0.28	0.21	0.12	0.10	0.12	-	-	-	1.23	449.0
Region VI	0.60	0.14	0.26	0.31	0.21	1.00	0.23	-	-	2.75	1,003.8
Region VII	0.64	0.32	0.17	0.42	0.30	0.23	1.06	-	-	3.14	1,146.1
Belém	0.55	0.40	0.25	1.61	0.14	0.25	-	-	-	3.20	1,168.0
Other Urban	0.61	0.88	0.28	0.17	1.06	0.27	0.26	-	-	3.53	1,288.5
Other Urban	0.82	0.15	0.28	0.25	0.26	0.34	0.86	-	-	2.96	1,080.4

a/ See Annex Table 14 for definition.
b/ Same items in the same order of importance as in Annex Table 15.

Source: ENDEF, FIBGE, 1978 based on "Consumo Alimentar Antropometria", Table 1; "Despesas das Famílias", Table 5; and Table 16.

TABLE 17

"MINIMUM" EXPENDITURE LEVELS - POVERTY LINES FOR REGIONS AND AREAS: BRAZIL (1974/75)

	Food Expenditure a/			Non-Food Expenditure b/			Total Expenditure Poverty Lines		
	A	B	C	A'	B'	C'	A+A'	B+B'	C+C'
REGION I									
Metropolitan Rio Janeiro	1,500	1,219	920	1,085	801	755	2,585	2,020	1,675
Metropolitan Rio Janeiro	1,586	1,328	954	1,238	913	861	2,824	2,241	1,815
Other Urban	1,257	766	877	829	611	576	2,086	1,377	1,453
Rural	917	649	637	603	445	419	1,520	1,094	1,056
Region II									
	1,473	919	972	1,190	878	827	2,663	1,797	1,799
Metropolitan Sao Paulo	1,710	1,146	1,076	1,664	1,227	1,157	3,374	2,373	2,233
Other Urban	1,290	664	911	909	670	632	2,199	1,334	1,543
Rural	1,126	762	784	627	463	436	1,753	1,225	1,220
Region III									
	1,129	876	720	756	557	525	1,885	1,433	1,245
Porto Alegre	1,623	1,168	846	1,270	937	883	2,893	2,105	1,729
Curitiba	1,256	1,084	904	989	729	687	2,245	1,813	1,591
Other Urban	1,208	835	766	860	635	598	2,068	1,470	1,364
Rural	955	817	643	571	421	397	1,526	1,238	1,040
Region IV									
Belo Horizonte	932	748	701	699	516	486	1,631	1,264	1,187
Belo Horizonte	1,293	682	863	989	729	687	2,282	1,411	1,550
Other Urban	979	660	797	796	587	553	1,775	1,247	1,350
Rural	858	846	620	683	504	475	1,541	1,350	1,095
Region V									
Salvador	969	668	723	651	480	453	1,620	1,148	1,176
Salvador	1,614	1,160	1,055	989	729	687	2,603	1,889	1,742
Recife	1,260	1,047	876	892	658	620	2,152	1,705	1,496
Fortaleza	1,067	1,058	802	812	599	564	1,879	1,657	1,366
Other Urban	975	894	836	820	605	570	1,795	1,499	1,406
Rural	879	449	619	498	368	347	1,377	817	966
Region VI									
	1,642	1,003	874	1,254	925	872	2,896	1,928	1,746
Region VII									
Belem	846	1,146	904	884	652	615	1,730	1,798	1,519
Belem	1,035	1,168	827	1,109	818	771	2,144	1,986	1,598
Other Urban	870	1,288	1,021	973	717	676	1,843	2,005	1,697
Other Urban	916	1,080	877	788	581	548	1,704	1,661	1,425
Areas									
Metropolitan	1,537	1,149	966	1,294	955	900	2,831	2,104	1,866
Other Urban	1,094	813	844	675	498	469	1,942	1,438	1,433
Rural	919	643	641	643	474	447	1,562	1,117	1,088
National Average	1,149	847	798	804	593	559	1,953	1,440	1,357

a/ Definitions of A through C - Basket A: Food items in proportion to their actual consumption at the 20th percentile of expenditure (monetary and non-monetary) distribution in each location, adjusted to provide the same national requirement of 2,242 calories per person daily (FAO/WHO); see [7]. Basket B: Major food items that actually provide 75% of calories per person in each location adjusted to meet location-specific requirements as in A. Basket C: Only cereals in their actual proportion in the average diet of each location, adjusted to give the same 2,242 calories per person daily as in A. B/ Multiplying national average food expenditures A through C by non-food/food expenditure ratio at the 20th percentile of current per capita expenditure distribution (i.e. 0.7), and the multiplying national non-food expenditure by non-food price index for the 40th percentile (Table 5), A' through C' are obtained.

Sources: Calculated from Tables 14, 17 and World Bank, Human Resources Special Report, October 1979, Annex III, Table 20.

TABLE 18

GINI COEFFICIENTS FOR REGIONS AND AREAS - BRAZIL

	1970 CENSUS [a]	1970 CENSUS [b]	ENDEF [c]
REGION I	..	.52	.47
Metropolitan Rio Janeiro	.54	..	.47
Other Urban	..	..	.40
Rural	..	..	.36
REGION II	..	.54	.44
Metropolitan São Paulo	.54	..	.44
Other Urban	..	..	.40
Rural	..	..	.41
REGION III	..	.49	.42
Porto Alegre	.52	..	.45
Curitiba	.51	..	.42
Other Urban	...	..	.41
Rural	..	..	.36
REGION IV	..	.54	.50
Belo Horizonte	.55	..	.52
Other Urban	..	..	.46
Rural	..	..	.44
REGION V	..	.56	.50
Salvador	.59	..	.50
Recife	.58	..	.50
Fortaleza	.59	..	.54
Other Urban	...	..	.46
Rural	..	..	.36
REGION VI	..	.49	.45
REGION VII	..	.46	.45
Belém	.56	..	.44
Other Urban	..	..	.45
Other Urban	..	..	.45
AREAS			
Metropolitan	..	..	.47
Other Urban	..	..	.43
Rural	..	..	.38

.. Not Available.

[a] Langoni [22] based on family income for 10 regions; translated for the ENDEF regions using population weights.

[b] Lodder [21], based on family income.

[c] Our estimates based on the ENDEF family expenditure.

Sources: Langoni [21], Lodder [22] and ENDEF [13].

TABLE 19

SPATIAL DISTRIBUTION OF POOR BASED ON A "CONSERVATIVE" DEFINITION OF POVERTY a/: BRAZIL (1974)

Regions	Poverty line a/ "Medium"	% Below	No. Below (1000)	Poverty Index b/	Income Deficiency c/
Region I d/	2,585	16.35	1,419	9.90	2.44
Metropolitan Rio Janeiro	2,824	13.88	991	9.68	2.46
Other Urban	2,086	17.78	186	9.57	3.39
Rural	1,520	31.33	276	11.74	3.84
Region II	2,663	20.79	4,333	8.13	1.61
Metropolitan Sao Paulo	3,374	13.82	1,148	7.51	1.52
Other Urban	2,199	13.28	939	9.11	2.65
Rural	1,753	20.59	697	10.42	4.36
Region III	1,885	18.96	3,364	7.74	1.88
Porto Alegre	2,893	14.93	237	5.75	0.79
Curitiba	2,245	10.54	85	5.92	1.09
Other Urban	2,068	16.73	972	8.48	2.47
Rural	1,526	18.00	1,607	8.38	2.45
Region IV	1,631	29.39	3,809	17.84	4.75
Belo Horizonte	2,282	18.57	340	9.89	2.11
Other Urban	1,775	21.14	1,093	10.05	1.19
Rural	1,541	40.83	2,431	24.08	10.19
Region V	1,620	48.01	13,903	25.91	9.97
Salvador	2,603	27.55	340	15.69	3.08
Recife	2,152	31.55	612	17.36	2.88
Fortaleza	1,879	36.24	388	22.98	4.36
Other Urban	1,795	38.13	3,189	24.99	10.67
Rural	1,377	54.78	8,967	24.44	15.79
Region VI	2,896	16.00	108	6.63	1.17
Region VII	1,730	14.35	526	12.68	2.75
Belem	2,144	20.75	154	13.53	4.52
Other Urban	1,843	27.63	306	19.07	6.34
Other Urban	1,794	12.22	259	6.96	1.12
Areas					
Metropolitan	2,831	17.38	4,403	10.41	2.18
Other Urban	1,942	22.63	6,944	13.64	4.52
Rural	1,562	39.36	13,978	18.65	10.06
National Average	1,953	29.36	27,462	15.45	5.05

a/ Based on the "medium" definition, (A+A') in Annex Table 17.
b/ Sen Index (I) in equation V.1 multiplied by 100.
c/ Equation (V.2) multiplied by 100.
d/ Note that calculations for regions made directly from ENDEF tables for the regions are not always obtained by adding up the sub-regions.

Source: Calculated from FIBGE (13) and Annex Tables 17 and 18.

REFERENCES

1. AHLUWALIA, Montek S., "Rural Poverty in India: 1956/57 to 1973/74", India Occasional Papers, World Bank, 1979.

2. ANAND, Sudhir, "Aspects of Poverty in Malaysia", Review of Income and Wealth, 23 No. 1, 1977.

3. BHALLA, Surjit, S., "Measurement of Poverty - Issues and Methods", Monograph, World Bank, January 29, 1980.

4. CAMPINO, Antonio C. C., "Custos de Programas de Suplementacao Alimentar no Meio Urbano", Revista Economica do Nordeste, Vol. 11, No. 2, April/June, 1980.

5. CAMPINO, Antonio C. C., "Situacao Nutricional no Brasil: Uma Descricao a Criticas as Estimativas do FIBGE", VII Encontro Nacional de Economia, ANPEC, Sao Paulo, December 1979.

6. COWELL, F. A., Measuring Inequality (Philip Allan, Oxford, 1977).

7. FAO/WHO Energy and Protein Requirements: Report of a Joint FAO/WHO Ad Hoc Expert Committee, FAO Nutrition Meeting Report Series No. 9 No. 521, WHO Technical Report Series No. 522 (Rome: 1973).

8. FONSECA, Marcos G. da, "Radiografia da Distribuicao Pessoal de Renda no Brasil: Uma Desagregacao dos Indices de Gini", Estudos Economicos, Vol. II, No. 1, January-March, 1981.

9. FUNDACAO GETULIO VARGAS, (FGV) Conjuntura Economica, Rio de Janeiro, various volumes.

10. FUNDACAO GETULIO VARGAS, (FGV) Pesquisas de Orcamentos Familiares, various volumes.

11. FUNDACAO INSTITUTO DE PESQUISAS ECONOMICAS (FIPE), Custo de Vida em Sao Paulo, Sao Paulo, various issues.

12. FUNDACAO INSTITUTO BRASILEIRO DE GEOGRAFIA E ESTATISTICA (FIBGE), Estudo Nacional da Despesa Familiar (ENDEF), Consumo Alimentar: Antropometria, Dados Preliminares, 7 volumes (Rio de Janeiro: 1977 and 1978).

13. FIBGE, ENDEF, Despesas das Familias, Dados Preliminares, 7 volumes (Rio de Janeiro: 1978).

14. FIBGE, Indicadores Sociais, Relatorio 1979 (Rio de Janeiro, 1979).

15. FIBGE, Inquerito Nacional de Precos (Rio de Janeiro: 1970).

16. HICKS, James F. Jr. and David M. Vetter, "Identifying the Urban Plan in Brazil", Draft Version, World Bank Research Proposal No. 672-37, Rio de Janeiro, Brazil, July 1981.

17. HOFFMAN, Rodolfo, "Tendencias da Distribuicao da Renda no Brasil e suas Relacoes com o Desenvolvimento Economico", in Tolipan, R. and A.C. Tinelli (eds.), A Controversia sobre Distribuicao de Renda e Desenvolvimento (Zahar Editores, Rio de Janeiro, 1975).

18. INSTITUTO DE PESQUISAS ECONOMICAS-INSTITUTO NACIONAL DE ALIMENTACAO (IPE-INAN), Avaliacao Global do Programa de Nutricao em Brasil, Second Report, October 1980.

19. KAKWANI, N.E. and N. Podder, "Efficient Estimates of the Lorenz Curve and Associated Inequality Measure from Grouped Observations", Econometrica, Vol. 44, No. 1, 1976.

20. KNIGHT, P.T., R. Moran, C. Lluch, D. Mahar and F. Swett, Brazil: Human Resources Special Report, The World Bank, Washington, D.C., 1979.

21. LANGONI, Carlos Geraldo, Distribuicao da Renda e Desenvolvimento Economico do Brasil (Editora Expressao e Cultura, Rio de Janeiro, 1973).

22. LODDER, Celsius A., Distribuicao de Renda nas Areas Metropolitanas, IPEA/INPES, Rio de Janeiro, 1976.

23. LLUCH, Constantino, "On Poverty and Inequality in Brazil" Draft, World Bank, May, 1981.

24. LLUCH, Constantino, Alan A. Powell and Ross A. Williams, Patterns of Household Demand and Savings, a World Bank Research Publication, Oxford University Press, 1977.

25. MACEDO, Roberto, "Salario Minimo e Distribuicao de Renda no Brasil", Estudos Economicos, Vol. II, No. 1, January-March 1981.

26. MALARD, Mayer, Maria Martha, "Comparasoes entre os Niveis de Precos nas Areas Metrapolitanes Abrangidas Pelo Sistema Nacional de Indices de Precos ao Consumidor" DESIP, IBGE, Rio de Janeiro, August 1981.

27. MEDEIROS, Paulo de Tarso, "Diferencas Geograficas no Custo de Vida", Rev. Bras. Econ., 31(2), 1977.

28. MUSGROVE, Philip, Consumer Behavior in Latin America, an ECIEL Study, Brookings Institute, Washington, D.C., 1978.

29. NATIONAL RESEARCH COUNCIL, Recommended Dietary Allowances, Eighth Revised Edition, 1974.

30. ORSHANSKY, M., "How Poverty is Measured", Monthly Labor Review, September, 1969.

31. PFEFFERMANN, Guy P. and Richard Webb, "The Distribution of Income in Brazil", World Bank Staff Working Paper, No. 356, September, 1979.

32. PRADO, Eleuterio F.S. and Roberto B.M. Macedo, Dimensao Regional da Pobreza: Um Reexame do Problema do Nordeste Brasileiro, A FIPE Research Project, Final Report, Sao Paulo, April, 1980.

33. PRADO, Eleuterio F.S., "Crescimento Economico, Probreza e Distribuicao de Renda em Paises Subdesenvolvidos", Estudos Economicos, Vol. II, No. 1, January-March, 1981.

34. REUTLINGER, S. and M. Selowsky, Malnutrition and Poverty, World Bank Occasional Paper No. 23, 1976.

35. SEN, A.K., "Levels of Poverty: Policy and Change", World Bank Staff Working Paper No. 401, July, 1980

36. SEN, A.K., "Poverty: An Ordinal Approach to Measurement", Econometrica, Vol. 44 (March 1976).

37. SEN, A.K. "Issues in the Measurement of Poverty", The Scandinavian Journal of Economics, Vol. 81, No. 2, 1979.

38. SOLORZANO, Cuadra Eduardo, "Diferencas Espaciais de Nutricao, Renda e Probreza no Brasil", Master's thesis, University of Sao Paulo, 1981.

39. SRINIVASAN, T.N., "Poverty: Some Measurement Problems", Conference Proceedings, Indian Statistical Institute Studies, No. 2, 1977.

40. SRINIVASAN, T.N., "Malnutrition: Some Measurement and Policy Issues", World Bank, 1979.

41. SUKHATME, P.V., "Malnutrition and Poverty", Ninth Lal Bahadur Shastri Lecture, Indian Agricultural Research Institute, 1977.

42. THOMAS, Vinod, "Spatial Differences in the Cost of Living", *Journal of Urban Economics*, 8, 1980

43. THOMAS, Vinod, "Spatial Differences in Poverty: The Case of Peru", *Journal of Development Economics*, 7, 1980.

44. U.S. DEPARTMENT OF HEALTH, EDUCATION AND WELFARE, *The Measure of Poverty* (Government Printing Office, Washington, D.C., 1976).

45. WILLIAMSON, Denise, "Food Prices and Consumption Comparisons - Brazil 1975", Unpublished Monograph (World Bank, 1981).

46. WORLD BANK, *World Development Report*, 1980.

DATE DUE

APR 1 7 1994			
APR 0 4 1994			
APR 2 8 1994			

DEMCO 38-297

BRAZIL
ENDEF REGIONS AND AREAS

IBRD-15975
SEPTEMBER 1981

- ⊛ NATIONAL CAPITAL
- • STATE AND TERRITORY CAPITALS
- STATE AND TERRITORY BOUNDARIES
- ENDEF REGIONAL BOUNDARIES
- INTERNATIONAL BOUNDARIES
- RIVERS

This map has been prepared by the World Bank's staff exclusively for the convenience of the readers of the report to which it is attached. The denominations used and the boundaries shown on this map do not imply, on the part of the World Bank and its affiliates, any judgment on the legal status of any territory or any endorsement or acceptance of such boundaries.